Only In America?

THE POLITICS OF THE UNITED STATES
IN COMPARATIVE PERSPECTIVE

Graham K. Wilson
University of Wisconsin–Madison

Chatham House Publishers, Inc.
Chatham, New Jersey

ONLY IN AMERICA?
The Politics of the United States in Comparative Perspective

CHATHAM HOUSE PUBLISHERS, INC.
Post Office Box One
Chatham, New Jersey 07928

PUBLISHER: Patricia Artinian
COVER DESIGN: Antler Designworks
MANAGING EDITOR: Katharine Miller
PRODUCTION SUPERVISOR: Melissa Martin
COMPOSITION: Bang, Motley, Olufsen
PRINTING AND BINDING: Versa Press, Inc.

LIBRARY OF CONGRESS CATALOGING-IN-PUBLICATION DATA
Wilson, Graham K.
    Only in America? : the politics of the United States in comparative perspective / Graham K. Wilson.
      p.   cm.
    Includes bibliographical references and index.
    ISBN 1-56643-058-5 (pbk.)
     1. United States—Politics and government. 2. National characteristics, American. 3. Comparative government. I. Title.
JK271.W58   1998
306.2'0973—dc21   98-8861
                                             CIP

Manufactured in the United States of America
10 9 8 7 6 5 4 3 2 1

Contents

Preface

T HE UNITED STATES arouses strong feelings. It is a country whose citizens are among the most patriotic in the world, convinced that their nation's political institutions and society are the most admirable. Yet the United States has also been the object of a torrent of criticism from other countries. The left in Europe long disdained it as the most capitalist of advanced industrial democracies, the nation in which business was least constrained by the state or unions; the American state was too weak to limit the power of business (even if it had wished to do so), and unions lacked the membership. European conservatives (until the 1970s) too were concerned with goals and values not well served by the market to approve of American society, and in consequence they tended to view the United States with disdain almost equal to the left's. Conservatives feared the consequences of mass culture (epitomized for them by Hollywood) unconstrained by elitism of the sort that brought Britain state-subsidized theater and the BBC and classical music. For the left, the masses in the United States were powerless in the face of the dominance of capitalism; for the conservatives, the masses were too powerful, producing a coarse, anti-intellectual, and culturally impoverished society. Both left and right agreed that the United States provided a dreadful warning, not a model, for the rest of the world.

Perhaps the late twentieth century has revealed a somewhat more nuanced picture. Europeans may know that in addition to McDonald's (which, after all, has been astonishingly successful in Europe), the United States produces outstanding symphony orchestras such as the Chicago Symphony and many internationally prominent opera singers. The European left has belatedly adopted many of the concerns of the American left: feminism, multiculturalism, environmentalism, and opposition to racism. Yet the belief persists that the United States is a very different and strange place. Even journalists working for "quality" British newspapers (as opposed to the "tabloids," which make no pretense of covering news intelligently) have difficulty in reaching beyond stereotypes of American politics and society. The British conservative weekly *The Spectator* recently stated sternly that the weird offerings of the United States to the rest of the world were moving beyond the tolerable (football) and were becoming increasingly unacceptable.[1] Other Europeans have even greater difficulty coming to terms with the United States. It has become fashionable to treat Britain and the United States as part of an allegedly "Anglo-Saxon" category[2] in comparative politics, a group of countries with low levels of protection for their citizens from the hardships of life.

The strong feelings that the United States arouses are the backdrop to this book, which approaches a topic that, for me, is both personally important and intellectually unavoidable. That topic is whether American politics is fundamentally similar to or different from politics in other advanced industrialized democracies. Among persons interested in the topic, this is known as the question of "American exceptionalism." This question, it cannot be stressed too strongly, is *not* whether the United States is "better" or "worse" than other nations but whether it is different.

This question has recurred throughout my teaching career. I started as a political scientist at the University of Essex in England teaching American politics. In mid career, I moved to the University of Wisconsin, where I taught mainly American politics, an area seen by most of its academic expositors as separate from and indeed possibly in competition or even conflict with comparative politics (although this was much less an issue at Wisconsin, in a department renowned for its collegiality and intellectual tolerance, than at many other universities). It was hard for me to see that someone who taught courses on American politics in England was a comparativist, while someone who taught the same courses in the United States was a different academic animal. More important, it seemed clear that the basic questions asked by comparative political scientists—what is distinctive about politics in any country, and why—were also appropriate to ask about American politics, even though they are rarely addressed explicitly or even implicitly by most experts on American politics.

As an Englishman living in the United States, married to an American, and making frequent visits to Britain, it was almost inevitable that I should be involved in numerous discussions at dinner parties about the nature of Americans and the United States compared with Europeans and European nations. Anyone who has been involved in such discussions will know how quickly they degenerate into stereotypes. Europeans quickly tell Americans that they live in a violent, selfish society that refuses to extend to its citizens the most basic forms of social protection (such as national health insurance), which are taken for granted by citizens of European nations. Discussion often becomes heated as Europeans explain these alleged features of American public policy in terms of the values of individual Americans. Motivated by a quest for individual advancement and success, Americans are said to be less willing than others to pay taxes to support the less fortunate. Americans sometimes give as good as they get, implying that they live in the only true democracy and the only society in which social mobility occurs. Only in America, they suggest, all evidence to the contrary notwithstanding, can someone from humble origins rise to the top.

Although European critics and patriotic American defenders of the United States disagree on much, they are united by the belief that the United States is indeed different. Visitors to the United States today, no less than in the nineteenth century, return to Europe with anecdotes, retold with a mixture of delight, astonishment, and horror, of what America is like. European social scientists have often felt obliged to treat the United States as the grand exception to theories in areas such as class conflict, voting behavior, and the development of the state. Contemporary theorists of American exceptionalism always sense the shadow of illustrious intellectual predecessors, particularly Alexis de Tocqueville,[3] Werner Sombart,[4] and perhaps most influential in this century, Louis Hartz.[5] In a variety of ways that we encounter later, these intellectual giants attempted to describe and explain a

United States that was dramatically different from other advanced industrial democracies. Yet a critical reading of their works inevitably prompts two questions.

The first question is whether the United States is indeed characterized by long historical continuities in its politics that make it unique. Those who believe in America's exceptionalism—the belief that the United States is fundamentally different in its politics from all other nations—assert that these fundamental differences can be traced back to the founding of the nation, if not earlier. Differences in social structure and ideology regarded as long established even by early-nineteenth-century visitors such as Tocqueville continue to shape American politics in a unique mold today. Yet we might doubt whether historical influences are so determining. The enormous changes in nearly all aspects of American life, including politics, over the past two hundred years make such stress on continuity questionable. Would the size and scope of government today or the nature of our political debates really seem familiar to Lincoln or his contemporaries?

The second question is whether American politics really is all that different from politics in other countries. Again, personal experience made me (belatedly) wonder whether the conventional account was true. After I had lectured for six years on American politics stressing the American traditions of hostility to high taxation, faith in market mechanisms, and antipathy to an extensive domestic role for the state (including doubts about a large-scale welfare state), I saw Britain enter into a period of Conservative, Thatcherite government that ended only when the left-of-center Labour Party adopted many of Thatcher's policies and repackaged itself as "New Labour." The key features of Thatcherite policy were, of course, hostility to high taxation, faith in market mechanisms, and antipathy to an extensive domestic role of the state (including doubts about a large-scale welfare state). The close parallels between the strategies of Tony Blair, the leader of the Labour Party, and President Clinton and his "New Democrats" are obvious. Books that I had treasured, such as Hartz's *The Liberal Tradition in America* and Samuel Beer's *British Politics in the Collectivist Age*[6] (or, as I knew it under its title in Britain, *Modern British Politics*) had long assured me of the fundamental differences between American and British conservatism. Yet the warm personal relations and policy cooperation between Margaret Thatcher and Ronald Reagan seemed to contradict any notion that these conservative leaders represented fundamentally different traditions. All the signs are that the relationship between Tony Blair and Bill Clinton is similarly close.

More important, I began to feel frustrated as a social scientist by the absence of evidence in discussions of America's exceptionalism. If you are asked to justify a claim that the politics of any country is fundamentally different from or similar to the politics of other countries, there are a number of obvious areas to explore. These include the nature of beliefs about politics and government, the issues that are the subject of political debate, patterns of public policy, and the character of political institutions. In other words, you would probably want to know whether people in a particular country held unusual beliefs about what government should do and how it should work, what issues were argued about in politics, what policies the government followed, and whether political institutions produced distinctive political practices or patterns of behavior.

On some aspects of the question of whether American politics is exceptional, evidence is fairly readily available; on others little research has been attempted. For example, eminent scholars have provided analyses of differences between the political beliefs of Americans and citizens of other democracies. Seymour Martin Lipset, for example, in numerous important and intriguing publications has argued that American political beliefs are very different from British or Canadian beliefs.[7] Contrarily, few if any efforts have been made to describe systematically what politics has been about in the United States, to summarize the content of the political agenda and compare it with the content of the political agendas of other democracies.

I believe that any verdict on how exceptional American politics really is should be based on analyses of all the areas mentioned earlier: beliefs, agendas, policies, and institutions. My book rests therefore on a mixture of discussion of original work by others and my own original work. I am very grateful to the scholars in this field whose works I cite, without which I could not attempt to provide an encompassing analysis of exceptionalism. I also wish to express my gratitude to the Glenn and Cleone Orr Hawkins benefaction to the Department of Political Science, University of Wisconsin, which has supported my research, and to my colleagues for making those resources available to me. Above all, I want to thank those who sparked my interest in American politics, especially the late Philip Williams, and those who have tolerated and assisted me in living a life anchored on both sides of the Atlantic Ocean. Prominent among these are my father Leslie Wilson, my wife Virginia Sapiro, and my son Adam Wilson, all of whom in different ways have accepted and assisted me in a peculiar lifestyle that reflects a reluctance to miss out on the glories of either European or American life.

I

Difference

This book is about whether politics in the United States is different from politics in other advanced industrialized democracies. Politics is always different to some degree from one country to another. Nevertheless, the belief has often been expressed that politics in the United States is so fundamentally different that the United States is "exceptional."

Exceptional—and the term naming the condition of being different from the norm, *exceptionality* or *exceptionalism*—are problematic words, however.[1] At the very least, they invite two additional questions. The first is, "How? In what respect is something exceptional?" If we say that something is exceptional, we have in mind general criteria for use in assessment, some explicit or implicit list of relevant characteristics. To say that a chocolate cake is exceptionally good indicates that we have expectations about the criteria for assessing chocolate cakes.

The second question is, "Compared with what?" With what or with whom are we making comparisons? If we say that a country's politics is exceptional, we are drawing a contrast between its politics and the politics of other countries, or at least other countries that we regard as being sufficiently similar in important respects, such as their level of economic development or their being commonly regarded as democracies, to make comparison meaningful. Thus if we are talking about Adam being exceptionally tall, it is important to know that we are comparing him with other twelve-year-olds, not players in the National Basketball Association.

What criteria are being used when we say that America's politics is exceptional, and with which countries' politics are we comparing America's politics? Unfortunately, there have not been uniform answers to these questions.

The first perspective on exceptionalism, the perspective that arouses the strongest passions, is the claim that the United States is exceptional in the degree to which it embodies such internationally espoused (if not universal) values as democracy, freedom, liberty, and, if only before the law, equality. This type of exceptionalism often appears in patriotic rhetoric. The United States is "the last best hope of mankind," a "city on a hill" that provides the rest of humanity with an example that they might aspire to emulate. The United States opened its arms to the downtrodden of the world, gave them equal treatment under the law, full citizenship rights, and the opportunity to succeed in life.[2]

The patriotic form of exceptionalism clearly contains an element of reality. Many immigrants to the United States from eastern Europe in the nineteenth century, as well as from countries such as Mexico today, have gained far greater political and citizenship rights by becoming American citizens than they would have enjoyed in their homelands. When Lincoln said at Gettysburg that the Union's dead in the Civil War had died so that "government of the people, by the people, for the people shall not perish from the earth," his implicit contrast was correct, although by the standards of the late twentieth century, vastly overstated. In spite of slavery and the denial—as in all other countries at that date—of citizenship rights to women, the United States was clearly more democratic than any other polity (including Britain).[3]

The success of struggles for democracy in other countries and the tremendous increase in the prosperity of Europe in the thirty years after World War II—trends that the United States generally tried its best to encourage—have made the contrasts between the degree of democracy in the United States and in other industrialized nations less dramatic than in Lincoln's day. Indeed, citizens of other democracies often believe that their systems are more, not less, democratic than the U.S. political system. Admirers of the British or Westminster model of democracy have argued that the type of parliamentary system it embodies is more democratic than the American system largely because of the clearer lines of accountability and responsibility of the governors to the governed that it embodies, aided by a considerably lesser role for money in politics. While patriotic Americans may point in reply to features of American politics such as stronger formal protection for civil liberties and legislation providing for greater public access to government information than Britons enjoy, the point is not who is right but that the question of which nation is more democratic is much harder to resolve today than in Lincoln's time.

This lessening of the contrasts between the United States and Europe is not limited to the political sphere but extends to aspects of social life such as prosperity and equality that have been interpreted as desirable consequences of American democracy. Europeans have become accustomed to levels of prosperity and mobility that would once have been associated only with the United States. Descendants of Italian immigrants to the United States may contrast their life in America with the lives of forebears in villages in Sicily; the contrast with Italians who moved to the north of Italy, one of the world's richest regions, is much less clear. Early-nineteenth-century observers thought that the United States exhibited unusually high levels of social equality, but at the end of the twentieth century the United States has one of the world's most unequal distributions of income and wealth.

Arguments about whether western European nations are more or less democratic than the United States occasionally provide some interesting insight into differences in how concepts such as democracy are understood. L.J. Sharpe, for example, argued that an important difference between British and U.S. understandings of democracy was that Americans tended to emphasize opportunities for participation, whereas the British tended to stress opportunities for the majority to be able to achieve its goals.[4] More commonly, such arguments produce more heat that insight. Non-Americans are deeply offended by Americans' claims of democratic superiority and respond by overemphasizing discredited aspects of American politics such as its dependence on vast amounts of money, low turnout in elections, and corruption. Although the work of some social scientists might seem to provide evidence relevant to these arguments, such as claims that Americans are more participatory than people in other democracies,[5] most who write on exceptionalism seek to escape the heavy emotional entanglements of debates over claims of national superiority. Seymour Martin Lipset, for example, one of the most important contemporary writers on the subject, carefully explains that when he writes of exceptionalism, he is not arguing for the superiority of the United States, merely its difference. What form does that difference take, however? In practice, different aspects of exceptionalism have been emphasized.

Culture

One of the most important forms of the argument for America's exceptionalism contends that Americans' values are exceptional. Americans have political goals different from those of citizens of other democracies, differing in what they expect from government, how they expect to be treated by government, and how they think government should behave. The commonly accepted view is that Americans hold beliefs that are summarized as falling within the "liberal tradition." Here the word *liberal* is used in its nineteenth-century, rather than contemporary, sense to mean belief in a limited role for government, protection of civil liberties, and democracy. If this view is correct, Americans expect less of government in services, particularly in the provision of social welfare, than do citizens of other democracies; they strongly support civil liberties such as freedom of the press; and they are of course strongly in favor of a democratic form of government.

The most influential expression of the belief that American politics takes place within a "liberal tradition" was provided by Louis Hartz. His book *The Liberal Tradition in America,*[6] by both describing and seeking to explain the dominance of a liberal tradition, did more than any other work to shape the debate over America's exceptionalism in modern times. Hartz argued that the liberal tradition was so strong in the United States that it was "hegemonic." Alternative schools of political thought that advocated a greater and more positive role for government could not thrive in the United States as they did in the countries of western Europe, Australia, New Zealand, and, to a more limited degree, Canada, because of the dominance of liberal thought. Chief among the political traditions that have been strong elsewhere but almost absent from American politics has been social democracy. The United States is unique among industrialized democracies in never having had a social democratic movement with a strong popular following. The question asked by the German sociologist Werner Sombart early this century, "why is there no socialism in the United States?"[7] has continued to preoccupy distinguished scholars such as Lipset.[8] It is important to stress, however, that Hartz noted the absence

4

from American politics not only of socialism on the left but also of paternalistic conservatism on the right, which, like democratic socialism, accepted a positive role for the state. Whereas British Conservatives and continental European Christian Democratic parties speedily accepted the creation of a welfare state that included government-funded health care, American conservatives have never accepted the legitimacy of the welfare state; congressional Republicans in the 1990s vehemently opposed the creation of national health insurance and vigorously pushed measures to restrict access to welfare for the poor.[9]

Hartz's book explored attitudes about the role of government in the thinking of politicians and intellectuals. We also have available a vast quantity of evidence gathered through opinion polls about the views of ordinary Americans. In a later chapter we use this evidence to ask whether in fact Americans do adhere to the liberal tradition that Hartz described. Are expectations about the appropriate role of government really as circumscribed as Hartz suggested? And are Americans unusually supportive of civil liberties such as freedom of expression for unpopular minorities, as the liberal tradition would require?

Agendas and the Content of American Politics

Between citizens and policies stand numerous institutions that have the capacity to transmit or distort their views. Institutions, as political scientists have long argued, admit interests (and opinions) to the political agenda or keep them off.[10] One argument made to explain the failure of social democracy in the United States is that the early development of mass political parties in the United States blocked the growth of a party with mass support among the working class; American (white male) workers were already committed to the Republican or Democratic parties before socialism had a chance to take root.[11] Some interests are likely to find it easier to place their concerns on the political agenda because of the way political institutions are organized. The fact that Congress continues to have agriculture committees in an era in which only about 2.5 percent of the population are farmers makes it easier for farmers to place their concerns on the political agenda.

Those who believe that the United States is exceptional would expect to find that its political agenda is distinctive. In particular, we would expect to find that the political agenda is dominated by issues that fit easily within a liberal tradition, whereas issues incompatible with such a tradition would be absent. Issues related to the welfare state would be relatively few, whereas issues related to civil liberties or civil rights would be more numerous. The relative weakness of support for social democratic concerns (such as building the welfare state) may also have left the United States more open to what have been termed "new politics" concerns, such as environmental protection. Ronald Inglehart argues that as levels of prosperity have increased, political attention has shifted from "bread and butter" issues such as the economy to concerns such as environmental protection.[12] The fact that the United States has one of the highest standards of living in the world should make it particularly likely to have a political agenda containing numerous "new politics" issues.

Although there is much theorizing about the political agenda and its biases, as we see later, there may be as much difficulty in defining it as in describing it. Is an item on the political agenda if it is discussed in Congress or one of its committees, or if it is mentioned by the president? In chapter 3 we explore further what it might mean to say that an issue is "on the political agenda" and examine whether the American agenda has been distinctive compared with the political agendas of other nations.

Policies

If, as Hartz argued, Americans believe in a more restricted role for government than do their counterparts in other democracies, and if the United States is a democracy, we would expect to find that government in the United States plays a smaller role in the lives of its citizens than do governments in other democracies. The United States would be exceptional, therefore, in terms of what its government does and fails to do, as well as in terms of the opinions of its citizens.

At first sight, as we detail in a later chapter, these expectations are fulfilled. Governments in the United States (national, state, and local) spend and control a smaller proportion of the gross domestic product (GDP) than governments in any other advanced democracy except Japan. The proportion of GDP spent and distributed by government in the United States is between a third and a quarter of the average proportion of GDP spent or controlled by other governments in the rich democracies' club, the Organization for Economic Cooperation and Development (OECD). The failure of American government to guarantee access to health care to all citizens in a national health insurance program is one of the most striking examples of the differences that underlie these figures. The United States is the only advanced industrialized democracy except Japan that does not have national health insurance or a national health service. When the United States does maintain programs like those that are part of the welfare state in other countries, it provides less generous support for a shorter period. American unemployment insurance, for example, pays the unemployed worker a much smaller fraction of lost income and for a shorter period than France, Germany, or the northern European social democratic welfare states provide.[13]

The arguments that public policy in the United States is "exceptional" are given closer scrutiny in a later chapter. All that we need note here is that it is at least plausible that government in the United States is exceptional in terms of the policies it follows. In particular, the United States has failed to develop a welfare state comparable to those found in nearly all other advanced industrialized democracies. In consequence, American government controls and spends a lower proportion of gross national product.

Institutions

The political institutions of the United States are highly distinctive. Parliamentary systems of government abound elsewhere in the world and can be divided into various categories; no other advanced industrialized democracy has emulated the American system, which Richard Neustadt characterized so well as "separated institutions sharing powers."[14] Even other presidential systems, such as France, have little in common with American institutions.

It is clear that American institutions are exceptional. Yet differing institutions can sometimes produce similar patterns of politics. The claim often advanced that American political institutions are prone to deadlock because of the separation of powers can be matched by examples from parliamentary systems such as Italy or Belgium, where deadlock can result from the inability of parties in coalition governments to agree on important issues.[15] A similar example is pork-barrel politics, the use of government programs or projects to buy political support. American politicians have been accused of resorting to the pork barrel in order to increase their chances of reelection and of trading pork-barrel favors in order to win votes in Congress for controversial legislation. Yet the pork barrel is not, as is commonly suggested, uniquely American. Pork-barrel politics helps explain the long dominance of the Liberal Democratic Party in Japan. British governments, operating in a very different institutional setting, have been said to practice pork-barrel politics in policies as varied as subsidizing agriculture and building the Humber bridge. In short, the fact that American institutions are unique does not guarantee that the patterns of politics they exhibit are necessarily unique. Chapter 4 explores whether the unique forms of American institutions have produced exceptional politics.

Theories of Exceptionalism

Let us for the moment assume, as most social scientists accept, that American politics is exceptional. Why should this be, and are the differences from politics elsewhere likely to persist? Just as we have distinguished different forms of exceptionalism, so we may distinguish different explanations.

Sociological Explanations

An obvious possible explanation for America's exceptionalism is that American society is unique. Politics reflects the society in which it is embedded, and American political exceptionalism is therefore a consequence of American social exceptionalism.

The most obvious feature of American society that has been used to explain its exceptionalism is its wealth. Sombart accounted for the weakness of socialism in the United States in part by saying that it had been buried in an avalanche of roast beef and apple pie; American workers in the nineteenth century were dramatically better off than their European counterparts, and at a time when mass immigration was occurring, many workers knew this. Yet wealth alone does not explain exceptionalism. Wealth can prompt resentment; resentment can fuel socialism. The United States is a country in which the distribution of wealth is unusually unequal. The wealthiest 1 percent of the population of the United States owns 39 percent of the nation's wealth; in contrast, the wealthiest 1 percent of the French population owns 25 percent of the nation's wealth, and the wealthiest 1 percent of the British population owns only 18 percent of that nation's wealth.[16]

It is of considerable importance, therefore, that there has also been a widespread belief in the United States that the country offers an unusually high level of social mobility, that people born to parents of modest means have a greater likelihood than their counterparts in other countries of rising to higher-paid, higher-status occupations. Studies of social mobility in advanced industrial countries have suggested that actually there is little difference in the rates of social mobility between the United States and countries such as Britain.[17] Nevertheless, Americans continue to believe that they live in "the land of opportunity," where social mobility is unusually prevalent, and this conviction is more important politically than the actual levels of mobility described by sociologists.

Another aspect of social class that has diminished political significance in the United States is the visibility of class divisions. Differences in how people speak, eat, dress, and behave are less linked to social class in the United States than in, for example, Britain. This contrast causes American journalists covering Britain to conclude that that country has a much more class-divided society than the United States. Accents in Britain are a sign of social class; in the United States, they are either regional or a reflection of one's position in the ethnic array. Working-class Britons eat their main meal in the middle of the day and call it dinner, while higher-class Britons eat dinner in the evening; in the United States, no such differences exist. Working-class Britons watch soccer (except in Wales and parts of northern England) when they follow professional sports; higher-class Britons watch rugby and tennis.

There are of course major differences in lifestyle in the United States associated with social class. Working-class Americans are more likely to smoke and to be overweight, for example, than professional-class Americans. In general, however, social class is less directly experienced in the United States than in Britain. Sombart noted a similar phenomenon in late-nineteenth-century America. Contrasting the United States with Germany, he was impressed by how much less visible (for example, in dress) were class divisions in the United States.[18]

Letters and diaries of English immigrants who came to mine lead in Mineral Point, Wisconsin, welcomed living in a world without deference in which they were not expected to doff their hats to the squire. Similarly, Lawrence Fuchs quotes an English immigrant to New Jersey who delighted in both a higher standard of living in the United States and the weaker sense of social hierarchy: "To us, who have long been half starved in England, it appears like a continuous feast . . . no fawning, cringing adulation here: the squire and the mechanic converse as familiarly as weavers do in England. We call no man master here."[19]

No matter how plausible these accounts are in explaining the past, it is far from clear that they reflect the present. The accumulation of vast fortunes in nineteenth-century America soon made the egalitarian world experienced by our English immigrant and described by Tocqueville a powerful folk memory, rather than a description of reality. Nor has the United States remained distinctive in terms of its prosperity. Although the United States still boasts one of the highest standards of living in the world, it is no longer clearly in advance of many western European countries in that regard. Neither is it always the case that, as is commonly supposed, economic prosperity helps the right and weakens the left. The decades since the oil shocks of the 1970s and the present day have coincided with a period of conservative dominance in American politics. Moreover, the enormous contrasts between rich and poor in the United States make it misleading to focus simply on high average incomes. The United States has a large number of people in poverty or on the verge of poverty—many of whom would clearly be better off materially if they lived in similar circumstances in a European welfare state—for whom the idea of an affluent society united in common consumption patterns is a mirage.

Meanwhile, although social class in Europe remains important, its manifestations have become more subtle. The traditional upper-class accent in Britain is more a disadvantage than an advantage, and regional accents are even acceptable to the BBC. An American observer who has known Britain well for over forty years remarked that when he first visited London, the crowds did indeed contain workers in blue overalls and executives from banks in the "City" uniform of a pin-striped suit and bowler hat; such sharp contrasts have given way to a Britain where everyone seems to shop at the same department store. All classes expect to own their own house, have central heating, vacation in other countries, and of course possess a car and a phone.[20]

Europe has followed the United States in retaining social classes but making class distinctions less visible.

One final obvious feature of American society is noted by all observers of exceptionalism. The United States is a country created by immigration (including, in the case of African Americans, forced immigration). The possible consequences of this obvious fact, which might explain exceptionalism, are numerous. First, self-selection might incline immigrants to the liberal tradition. Those most interested in self-advancement emigrate; those interested in collective action to raise living standards do not. Second, immigration provided the basis for a national myth (and myths contain at least an element of truth) in which the United States was seen as, in Fuchs's words, "an asylum in which *liberty, opportunity,* and *reward for achievement* [original emphasis] would prosper."[21] These attributes were clearly antagonistic to the development of a strong welfare state that would promote equality through the redistribution of income and wealth. Third, although Americans are often urged to "celebrate difference," the reality is that members of relatively homogeneous societies are more likely to support each other in need through the creation of a welfare state. The belief that "they"—a racially or ethically different group—behave in a way that undermines the case for giving them assistance diminishes support for welfare state measures. The African American unmarried mother living on welfare is perhaps the most commonly cited example of this phenomenon.

Cultural Explanations

It was Richard Hofstadter who argued that the fate of Americans has been "not [to] have an ideology but to be one."[22] As numerous commentators have noted, it is possible to talk about American beliefs or the American political tradition in a way that it is impossible to talk about French beliefs or British beliefs; the overwhelming majority of Americans subscribe to a core set of beliefs about how society ought to be organized. These core values were discussed briefly earlier: equality before the law, democracy, civil liberties, a limited role for government in pursuing social equity or prosperity, and a strong dependence on the fairness and efficiency of market mechanisms. People who dissent from these core values, such as socialists, have frequently suffered persecution in the United States. Socialists were harassed in the 1940s and 1950s by various arms of the state, including the revealingly titled Committee on Un-American Activities of the House of Representatives. The thought of a committee of the National Assembly in France investigating un-French activities is farcical; would it have examined refusals to eat good bread or to drink wine? The House Un-American Activities Committee in the United States was in no doubt of its mission: to examine the activities of those who dissented from the American creed.

It is very plausible to argue, therefore, as did Louis Hartz, that American politics is shaped and confined by the hegemony of what he termed the "liberal tradition." The crucial fact about American politics is that it does not have the range of views found in the politics of most other democracies. There is no socialist or communist left, as in France and Italy, nor have there been any explicitly antidemocratic parties of the far right.

Many objections have been raised to Hartz's arguments. Most of them are discussed in the next chapter. We should note here, however, that some political scientists object to any explanation of politics in terms of political culture. The issue is whether cultural interpretations of politics really explain why politics is the way it is or merely describe politics further. Critics of interpreting a nation's politics in terms of culture simply transpose the question: what causes a nation's culture to be the way it is? Moreover, cultural interpretation runs the risk of being circular; we say that American politics is exceptional because of American culture, and thus we are able to describe American political culture by looking at American politics. We use the same evidence both to describe and to explain what makes American politics unique. The arguments against cultural explanations—and the replies that can be made to these arguments—are discussed in the next chapter.

Institutionalist Explanations

While cultural explanations of politics are less fashionable than they used to be, "institutionalist" explanations are more popular than they have been for decades. Institutionalists explain policy outcomes in terms of the patterns of political behavior that are encouraged or discouraged by the institutions in which political activity occurs. Sven Steinmo has argued that the major distinctive feature of American government—its relatively small scale—is a consequence of American political institutions.[23] The separation of decisions about taxing and spending in particular (except in the case of Social Security) encourages hostility to government because Americans are not encouraged to consider the benefits they derive from government in conjunction with the taxes it imposes on them. Americans tell opinion pollsters that they want more spending on almost every type of policy. Government in the United States is perpetually short of money, however, because the legislators who make decisions on taxation are responsive to political pressures from those who want tax breaks and are not counter-pressured by those who want to strengthen government programs.[24]

Terry Moe makes another argument that institutions shape our experience of government. A standard complaint about government in the United States is its inefficiency. Such complaints may be exaggerated; as James Q. Wilson shows, many government agencies in the United States work very well.[25] Moe, however, argues that many agencies are doomed to inefficiency and delay because they have been designed not to achieve their supposed goals effectively but to strike a compromise between supporters and opponents of the policy in question; the Occupational Safety and Health Administration (OSHA) operates within a framework designed not to promote efficiency but to embody a bargain struck between supporters and opponents of federal regulations on workplace safety and health.[26]

Moe's argument that American institutions produce policy bargains, rather than efficiency, could be taken even further. Many—perhaps most—policy areas in the United States provide examples of concessions made to powerful lobbies that detract from the overall fairness and efficiency of the program. The tax system has generally been loaded with special exemptions and allowances that have no basis in equity or efficiency. Even conservative Republican politicians such as Senator John Warner of Virginia boast of their success in winning federal funds for their states or districts, arguing that if they do not bring home the pork, some other legislator will.[27] Getting elected, or winning support for legislation in Congress, involves making deals on policy issues that have little substantive justification. Policy inequity and administrative inefficiency are inevitable consequences of the maneuvers forced on American politicians by the institutional system in which they operate. If Americans distrust their state, it can be argued, their institutions have given them good reason.

Yet at the end of the day there is something troubling about explaining politics entirely in terms of institutions. Most of us most of the time do take institutions for granted. If we were totally dissatisfied with institutions and their consequences, however, would we not at some point change them? Nations do adapt and change their institutions when the demand to do so is strong enough. National emergencies such as the Civil War, the Great Depression, or World War II resulted in very rapid changes in American institutional capacities. Attempts to graft alien institutions onto societies rarely succeed; the Westminster-style democracies that Britain had created in its former African colonies all quickly disappeared after it gave them independence. It seems implausible to suppose that institutions alone can explain politics.

Path Dependency

The final perspective on exceptionalism suggests in a way that there is no such thing as exceptionalism because every nation follows a unique trajectory. Where political systems end up depends in large part on where they start out. Nations today necessarily develop in different ways because they start out in different places. A nation continues along a path today not because it is ideal but because it is the continuation of the path it has taken in the past, and the costs of changing paths would be very high. Only rare and momentous events such as a revolution or losing a war force nations to change direction. The rest of the time, the natural tendency is to continue along the path of the past.

Political scientists such as Paul Pierson[28] who emphasize the importance of path dependency in politics point to numerous factors that make radical change unlikely. First, past commitments do much to shape current government budgets and programs. As Richard Rose has argued, inheritance comes before choice in public policy.[29] The vast majority of government spending and activity flows from decisions made by politicians previously, not currently. Politicians and administrators may find it difficult to imagine alternative approaches to those they are used to, and shifting from one policy approach to another may be very costly in terms of the administrative and legislative effort required. Perhaps most important, past commitments create contemporary political pressures. Those who have paid into the Social Security System would be furious if it were abolished; the fact that we have created a vast health-care industry that is privately owned creates powerful pressure groups that oppose a government-financed system like those that exist in all industrialized democracies other than the United States.

Though plausible, path dependency, like all other explanations of exceptionalism we have encountered, has its problems. In the first place, the notion of a "path" that nations follow is imprecise. As when taking a hike in woods, it is sometimes difficult to know whether one is on or off the path. Consider as an example the creation of Social Security in the 1930s. Was the development of Social Security a radical departure on a new path, or was it a development of older ideas and policies? Most political scientists and historians have seen Social Security as a radical new departure in which the federal government assumed unprecedented responsibilities for providing for the needs of its citizens. Yet Theda Skocpol suggests that the United States had been an innovator in pension policies, developing pension programs by the early twentieth century (for mothers and soldiers) that were on a greater scale than pension programs in other countries at that time.[30] Clearly, which side one takes in this debate will determine whether or not one thinks that the creation of Social Security took the United States on a new path. Similarly, while scholars using the notion of path dependency allow for the occurrence of critical events that produce sharp changes in direction, it is hard in practice to identify these and to distinguish them from striking out on a new path.

A more fundamental objection to path dependency is that it ignores the fascinating tendency for nations to develop in similar ways at particular historical moments. The wave of democratization that swept the world in the early 1990s is a case in point. Less dramatically, the policies followed by Margaret Thatcher in Britain from 1979 onward (cutting government expenditures on social programs, cutting taxes on incomes, shrinking the size and scope of government) were soon matched by similar developments in the United States under President Reagan, in the Netherlands, and even under social democratic governments in Australia and New Zealand. Most advanced industrialized democracies moved toward creating welfare states at a similar historical moment, and most have been more sensitive to issues of individual freedom and civil liberties in recent decades. Instead of imagining each nation as moving along a unique path, we might imagine advanced industrialized democracies as ships in a convoy. Some are ahead of others or off to either side; all are progressing in the same general direction.

Characterizing American Politics

A striking feature of theories of America's exceptionalism is the confidence of their authors that the United States really is an exceptional case. As we later see, the validity of this conviction is less obvious than most assume. The purpose of this book is to challenge the assumption that the United States is dramatically different from other advanced industrial democracies. To do so, we look at several ways in which politics is described in order to make the exceptionalists' case. These are the beliefs of Americans, the content of the American political agenda, the size and scope of government in the United States, and the consequences of American political institutions. We commonly encounter the paradox of whether the glass is half empty or half full: often there is no hard test of whether differences between nations are significant or insignificant. My purpose, however, is to show that there is more liquid than is commonly supposed in a glass assumed to be all but empty.

2

Cultural Interpretations
of American Politics

S WE SAW in chapter 1, one of the most popular interpretations of American politics is that it is confined
within what Hartz called the "liberal tradition." The
historical experience of the United States resulted in the
deep implantation of a liberal tradition that stressed the importance of
individual property rights and political rights. Other modern ideologies of the left[1] or right that placed less emphasis on individual property rights or political rights failed to attract a mass following. The
fact that the United States was created too late in history to experience
feudalism precluded the establishment of a paternalistic conservative
tradition, an ideology associated with a hereditary upper class. The
extension of citizenship rights, so speedy that by the 1830s nearly all
white males had the right to vote irrespective of their income or
wealth, precluded the creation of a socialist movement with extensive
popular appeal.

Hartz thus provided an account of the "exceptional" character of
American politics, an explanation of why the United States alone
among the developed democracies has no significant labor or social
democratic party, and why the U.S. government provides less for its
citizens than governments in any stable democracy other than Japan.

In this chapter, we return to Hartz's cultural analysis of American
politics, subjecting it to more detailed criticism.

Can There Be a Cultural Explanation of Politics?

The first issue to address is whether there can be a cultural explanation of politics anywhere. Once, cultural approaches to politics seemed firmly entrenched. Not only Hartz's discursive historical approach but survey-based research such as Gabriel Almond and Sidney Verba's more tightly defined and comparative study, *The Civic Culture,* assumed the importance of ideas and attitudes in shaping politics.[2] Since then, a series of vigorous attacks have been launched on studies that assert the importance of cultures in shaping politics. The major criticisms focus on alleged circularity or triviality of cultural interpretations and the greater significance of other factors, such as political institutions, in shaping public policy.[3]

The alleged circularity of cultural approaches lies in using observations to explain the existence of the culture that are then used as examples of the results of the political culture. We might, for example, suggest that the absence of national health insurance in the United States—long established in every other advanced democracy—is evidence of a unique American political culture that attaches little value to the collective provision of health care for all because of the culture's individualistic character. The absence of national health insurance might be explained, however, by the existence of an individualistic political culture that attaches little significance to the provision of collective benefits such as guaranteed access to health care for all. The same fact is both the explanation and that which is to be explained.

A similar criticism suggests that culture itself is not an explanation but merely a reflection of some deeper factors on which we should focus. In crude Marxism, for example, ideologies were seen simply as a product of class arrangements that they served to legitimate; in every period the dominant ideas are the ideas of the ruling class. Less dialectically, political cultures are the results of current or historical experiences. We gain more by focusing on the circumstances that have produced the ideas than on the fact that people hold them. Thus if Mexicans, as Almond and Verba claimed, view the police and government officials as idle, corrupt, and frequently brutal, the reasons why this is a plausible account of Mexican government are more important than the fact that Mexicans hold these attitudes. We might say that political culture is remembered collective experience (such as recurring dangers of persecution for Jews), but why bother to introduce political culture as a mediating, complicating factor between experience and current behavior?

There are several answers to these objections.

First, the fact that something is caused by something else does not make it useless as an explanatory factor itself. Attitudes shaped by circumstances can have an independent effect, even after the situation that gave rise to them has ended. Anti-Semitism may well have declined in the United States, but the collective memory of Jews sustains attitudes such as a concern for civil liberties that anti-Semitism provoked. Just as institutions created in response to pressures, interests, and concerns at a particular moment may thereafter have an independent and continuing impact on politics, so a political culture, once created, may shape thinking about politics. This is particularly likely to be the case in a nation such as the United States in which, as noted in chapter 1, conceptions of national identity are intertwined with ideology. In a nation in which, within the experience of many living Americans, to hold beliefs that were outside the mainstream was to invite social ostracism or even persecution by government agencies and employers for being "un-American," we need not be surprised to find that most people continue to interpret their needs and experiences through a dominant ideology.

Second, few political scientists today would be so purely materialist as to suggest that social experiences translate into political thought or action without being influenced by preconceptions about politics and society. The same experience, such as losing a job, can be interpreted in a variety of ways depending on what beliefs the unemployed person holds about the economy and society. For some, unemployment is an unfortunate but transient experience perhaps due to mistakes of politicians in an otherwise just market system; for others, the experience is proof of the viciousness of capitalism. Marxists once asserted the primacy of material conditions in shaping political behavior and thought. Perhaps the continuing unwillingness of the masses to behave as Marx had prescribed made later Marxist theorists recognize the importance of the construction of political meaning. Peasants and workers who failed to rebel were often deemed victims of "false consciousness." Though presumptuous in its willingness to tell people how they ought to think politically, such analysis at least demonstrated an awareness of the importance of beliefs, cultures, and traditions in politics. Beliefs can indeed obscure reality; even while evidence mounts that the United States is the most unequal society among the advanced democracies in terms of the distribution of wealth and income, Americans continue to believe that they live in an unusually egalitarian setting.

Finally, even if political culture were to be thought merely a product of deeper social forces, what in Marxist circles was termed an epiphenomenon, it would not follow that it was uninteresting. If we believe, for example, that political culture merely reflects the values and interests of a dominant group, it is worth examining political culture as a clue to what the character of the dominant group or class is. Shifts in a political culture might provide valuable clues about shifts in power relations in a society, such as the emergence of a more powerful bourgeoisie.

We may conclude, in short, that political culture is still worth studying, even for those who doubt that political ideas are a powerful influence on political behavior. Political culture is at least either an interesting manifestation of the power of dominant social groups or a mediating factor standing between material events or experiences and political behavior. More probably, political culture influences how we interpret and respond to events.

Ambiguity and Contradiction

Another line of attack on the value of political culture accepts that it is interesting but asserts that it is too confused and complex to be worth studying. This criticism takes many forms.

There are of course important divisions between those who believe in the efficacy of survey research as a guide to political culture and those who do not. For some political scientists, the answers to carefully designed survey questions reveal the underlying beliefs and attitudes of respondents. For others, such questions represent an imposition of concepts and choices on citizens whose political beliefs or modes or reasoning are not necessarily those of the person who designed the questions. This methodological division often coincides with a disagreement about the capacity of mass publics to hold complex, interrelated beliefs. Ever since Philip Converse's highly influential work,[4] many political scientists have argued that mass publics hold disconnected and often contradictory beliefs. The mass public is therefore illogical in its reflexes, perhaps because only elites think seriously about politics. At times these apparent contradictions may be merely the result of a lack of thought. At other times, however, such a contradiction may reflect considerable ambivalence about the concept itself, making its application highly dependent on circumstances. Americans have been said to be strong believers in equality in some situations (legal equality, equality of opportunity) and strongly opposed to equality in other circumstances (equality of wealth or income). Which of these themes will be evoked in a particular situation may be difficult to predict depending on whether the situation is presented in terms of "unfair" advantage or disadvantage.

These ambivalences in the general American political culture are complicated further by the ethnic, racial, and geographic diversity of the United States. No one should doubt the importance of divisions between white and black Americans in how they view the nation's race problems. As Donald Kinder and Lynn Sanders write, "the most arresting feature of public opinion on race is how emphatically black and white Americans disagree with each other."[5] Yet even on race, as Kinder and Sanders acknowledge, much may depend on the way in which the issues are framed in public debate.[6] To complicate matters further, evidence suggests that if we leave behind discussions of specific government programs or responsibilities about which there are indubitably important differences between black and white Americans[7] and focus instead on visions of what constitutes a good society, African Americans are not very different from Americans in general in their values. As Jennifer Hochschild writes:

> Americans are close to unanimity in endorsing the idea of the American dream.... Three fourths or more of both races agree that all people warrant equal respect, that skill rather than need should determine wages, that "America should promote equal opportunity for all" rather than "equal outcomes," that "everyone should try to amount to more than his parents did" and that they are ambitious themselves. Seventy percent of black and 80 percent of white Californians agree that "trying to get ahead" is very important in "making someone a true American." An even more overwhelming majority of black than white Americans endorse self-sufficiency as one of their primary goals.[8]

Closer to the realm of practical politics, however, the appeal of the idea that "the less government there is, the better" is greater among whites than among blacks.[9]

In contrast to the ambiguities about whether African Americans and whites have similar political beliefs, there is general agreement that clear differences exist between the political cultures of American regions. Beliefs about the appropriate role of government or appropriate standards of political behavior are noticeably different in Minnesota and Wisconsin than in Arkansas. Few would suggest that the South had the same political beliefs as the North; Louis Hartz struggled unconvincingly to provide an explanation of how the South could be said to share in a general, all-American liberal tradition when its society was characterized by hierarchy, slavery, and oppression. Yet the differences between American regions are not reducible to a simple "South versus North" division. Important contrasts exist within these regions as well as between them.

The historian David Fischer suggests that these differences are traceable through the ages to the original European settlements of the regions.[10] Settlers from different parts of England brought with them different political beliefs and attitudes that, once implanted, have continued to shape the politics of those regions. Fischer contends that four distinctive cultures were transplanted from England to the United States: the Puritan settlement of Massachusetts, the settlement in Virginia by English from "a broad belt of territory that extended from Kent and Devon north to Northamptonshire and Warwickshire," a settlement in the Delaware Valley dominated by the Friends from northern England, and a fourth migration from the borderlands of North Britain (northern England, the Scottish lowlands, and northern Ireland) into the "backcountry." "Each of these four folk cultures had a distinctive character," Fischer notes, and interacting with geography and other local circumstances, these cultures persisted, producing "at least four different ideas of liberty within a common cultural frame."[11] Is it really plausible to talk about a single American political culture, rather than several, or perhaps many, American political cultures?

Hartz argued that American politics was dominated by liberalism. But just as there are many American political cultures, so there are many variants of the ideology liberalism that Hartz associated with the United States. J. David Greenstone, for example, suggests that we differentiate between liberalisms that treat people's preferences as a given and those that aim at a transformation through social or political improvement.[12] Similarly, Richard Ellis argues that liberal traditions contain enough inner tensions and contradictions to avoid sterile consensus. "If Americans inhabit a social universe characterized by rival social biases, then they have plenty of opportunity to compare their bias with other biases. If alternative ways of looking at the world are constantly clashing, then there is plenty of scope for learning about testing and even abandoning cultural attachments. *Culture is a prism that biases the way one experiences the world, not a prison that shuts one completely off from that world.*"[13]

We know from watching arguments before the Supreme Court that the practical definition of core liberal values such as those embedded in the Bill of Rights is not easy. Is there a point at which free speech about sex degenerates into pornography demeaning to women? Reasonable people disagree. Not surprisingly, practices differ from country to country. The British are shocked by the threats to a fair trial posed by extensive pretrial publicity in the United States (showing their concern about the liberal value of securing the rights of the accused), while Americans insist on the freedom of the press to insinuate a defendant's guilt before a trial is held (thus defending freedom of the press). Is affirmative action reverse discrimination or action to compensate for past or present racism? Again, reasonable people disagree, and in so doing they disagree about the compatibility of affirmative action with core liberal principles such as treating individuals equally. We are profoundly mistaken if we think that even the most obvious core beliefs of liberalism somehow free us from political debate.

Indeed, the most striking feature of the history of liberalism in the United States is the elasticity of its principles. Thomas Jefferson, chief ideologist of the Declaration of Independence with its commitment to the "self-evident truth" that "All men are created equal," was a slaveholder, and several of his slaves had the good fortune to escape to the British during the War for Independence. More than 150 years later, American intellectuals and artists, such as the China specialist Owen Lattimore and the movie producer Sam Wanamaker, who had been hounded for their political beliefs by anticommunist politicians in the McCarthy era, also "escaped" to the British. Although less demonstratively committed in theory than Americans to core liberal values such as freedom of thought and speech, the British at the time were more committed to them in practice.

It used to be commonplace to argue that liberals were blind to the social problems that inhibit freedom or, indeed, make the existence of formal legal freedoms a mockery. Liberals were accused by socialists of defending the right of the individual to speak freely while not caring whether he had sustenance to give him the strength to do so. In fact, this criticism was never fair. Classic liberal theorists such as John Stuart Mill recognized that meaningful choice does not exist for those in poverty. Liberal governments such as Britain's great reforming administration of 1906–16 began the creation of the welfare state, and later liberal theorists such as T.H. Green provided theoretical underpinnings for the movement to create what became known as positive freedoms. Several decades later, Roosevelt included freedom from want in his list of the "Four Freedoms," which in December 1941 he pronounced to be the basis of any postwar settlement. Roosevelt's declaration demonstrated the acceptance in the United States that positive liberties were compatible with American liberalism, an acceptance implicit in much of his New Deal program. Thus it is quite untrue to say that liberals created merely formal freedom, disregarding social constraints on it.[14]

We are faced, therefore, with a real question about whether American liberalism is really as different from European social democracy as Hartz thought. American liberals have been vigorous defenders of expensive government programs such as Social Security, Medicare, and Medicaid that provide assistance to citizens, even though it is true that American liberals have never shown much enthusiasm for government ownership of industries (the Tennessee Valley Authority is one interesting exception). European social democrats, however, have themselves abandoned whatever commitment they had to ending capitalism by socializing industries. Never pursued by Swedish social democrats, the strategy of socializing industries was abandoned by German social democrats in the 1950s and, though in practice abandoned much earlier, by the British Labour Party in 1994 when it amended Clause IV of its constitution. It is plausible, therefore, to think of American liberals and European social democrats sharing a commitment to ameliorating social problems and reducing social inequality through government programs but within the context of a capitalist economic system that neither of them challenges. To make the differences between European social democrats and American liberals even more ambiguous, both have had their most effective periods when they have worked in alliance with labor unions. The creation of the Great Society programs in the 1960s was achieved with the strong support of the bulk of the union movement, and the turning back of conservative attacks on British government programs in 1996 was accomplished by a coalition of liberals and labor unions.

We might equally note that the contrast between American conservatism and European conservatism that Hartz emphasized is much less evident today than in the past. Hartz was clearly struck by the difference between conservatives in the United States, very hostile to the welfare state and government action to promote social equality, and British Conservatives, heirs to a tradition of accepting a larger, more active government to the point of even accepting the welfare state. British Conservatives seemed to follow aristocratic notions of *noblesse oblige* that the better off had the duty to protect the less-well-off, whereas American conservatives were individualists, much more thoroughgoing in their opposition to government programs. American conservatives, Hartz thought, were not believers in real conservatism at all. Real conservatives believed in notions of social solidarity. Society was like a body. Just as different limbs might have different functions and status but were linked one to another, so members of society were interlinked and interdependent.

Again, however, events have made the contrasts much less clear than Hartz suggested. Aristocratic notions of *noblesse oblige* gave way in Britain to the politics of Thatcherism. Under the leadership of Mrs. Thatcher, British Conservatives cut taxes and welfare and determinedly reduced the reach of the state. State-owned industries—including many often publicly owned in the United States, such as water supply and airports—were privatized. Any notions of social solidarity or of society's organic character were replaced with an emphasis on incentives and individualism that was very congenial to American conservatives; indeed, Mrs. Thatcher became the heroine of the American right. Just as American liberals and European social democrats had become harder to distinguish, much the same could be said of British and American conservatives. Indeed, even in France, where conservatism was particularly strongly associated with acceptance of a powerful state, right-of-center politicians such as Jacques Chirac pursued the familiar strategy of shrinking the size and scope of government, partly through an extensive program of privatization.

Hartz argued that in the United States the hegemony of the liberal tradition would keep off the political agenda ideas that would find their way onto it in other democracies, including Britain. We have seen that there are reasons to doubt that this is likely to be the case. The American political agenda may well be less restricted, therefore, than Hartz supposed. Perhaps, these reasons aside, Hartz was wrong in any case. Hartz has often been labeled a "consensus theorist" for arguing that American politics is confined within a liberal mold. Yet, as we have seen, a liberal mold does not end the opportunities for political disagreement. Fervent arguments take place about whether affirmative action is consistent with liberal values (by increasing opportunities) or inconsistent (because it does not treat individuals equally). Indeed, as Samuel Huntington has argued persuasively, agreement on values can promote conflict.[15] Allegations that shared principles are being ignored or compromised become common, particularly in periods of "credal passion." As Huntington notes, although conservative politicians hoped to find evidence that student activists in the 1960s were working on behalf of the Soviet Union, the reality was that they were motivated by traditional American values such as liberty, equality, and democracy. The very names of the major groups—Students for a Democratic Society, the Free Speech Movement—were reminders of how the "New Left" in the 1960s was motivated by traditional values. Yet the conflict between the New Left and its opponents could not be described as anything less than conflictual, far from the "consensual" politics that the liberal tradition was said to guarantee.

We may conclude, therefore, that interesting and plausible though theories such as Hartz's are, they are not necessarily correct in asserting that the American political agenda will be tightly constricted. What Hartz himself called the "liberal tradition" can produce formidable controversies, and in practice neither the left (liberals) nor the right (conservatives) in the United States are as different from their European counterparts as Hartz supposed. In the face of inconclusive though fascinating theories it is time to turn to the facts.

Evidence

If American political culture does not guarantee consensus on the application of core liberal principles such as freedom of speech or on the measures needed to provide sufficient "positive freedoms" such as freedom from want, does it have any importance in shaping our politics? Is American liberalism really an influence on our practical politics, or are the principles of liberalism sufficiently elastic that our politics can be much the same as in other democracies?

The answer at first glance appears to be clear. Americans do seem to hold attitudes that distinguish them from the citizens of most democracies, for example on the distribution of wealth and income. When asked by opinion pollsters whether it is the responsibility of the government to reduce the differences in income between people with high incomes and those with low incomes, Americans are much less likely to respond affirmatively than are people in other democracies. Similarly, Americans are much less likely to believe that it is the duty of the government to provide a guaranteed basic income.

	Government should reduce income inequality (% agreeing)	Government should guarantee a basic income (% agreeing)
Italy	80	69
Germany	66	58
Britain	65	66
Sweden	53	43
Canada	48	48
United States	39	34

SOURCE: ISPP polls as reported in *Public Perspective*, April/May 1995, 20.

Numerous other polls suggest that there is consistent and continuing support for the principles of the liberal tradition. In 1991, for example, the *Times/Mirror* conducted a survey of political attitudes in the United States and various European countries. One question was whether people agreed or disagreed with the statement that "it is the responsibility of the state [in the United States this phrase was changed to "the government"] to take care of very poor people who cannot take care of themselves." The percentage saying that they "completely agree" was dramatically lower in the United States than in any of the European countries surveyed.

Spain	71
Italy	66
Britain	62
France	62
West Germany	45
United States	23

SOURCE: *Public Perspective* November/December 1991, 5.

United States	34
Italy	14
Germany	13
France	10
Britain	9

SOURCE: *Public Perspective*
November/December 1991, 7.

Not surprisingly, the United States also differed from European countries in the percentage saying that they *disagreed* that "the state/government should guarantee every citizen food and basic shelter."

Austria	90
Italy	87
Britain	76
West Germany	76
Switzerland	68
Netherlands	66
Australia	61
United States	58

SOURCE: *Public Perspective*
March/April 1990.

In the distribution of income and wealth, the United States, according to recent studies, is one of the most inegalitarian of advanced nations. Although most Americans are concerned about income inequality, a lower percentage of Americans than of citizens of other countries find income inequality unacceptable. (The table reports the percentage that agreed or strongly agreed that differences in income are too large.)

Italy	82
Austria	81
Netherlands	65
Britain	64
West Germany	61
Australia	44
Switzerland	43
United States	29

SOURCE: *Public Perspective,*
March/April 1990.

Thus a small majority of Americans are concerned about income inequalities. But in reply to the proposition that "it is the responsibility of government to reduce the differences in income between people with high incomes and those with low incomes," few Americans strongly agreed or agreed that government had such a responsibility.

Tom W. Smith provided an interesting summary of differences in attitudes to the role of government in the United States and comparable democracies by creating an average level of support for or opposition to five statements about the welfare role of government. The five statements were that the government should

- "reduce differences in incomes between people with high incomes and those with low incomes";
- "provide a job for everyone who wants one";
- "spend less on benefits for the poor" (*strongly disagree/disagree*);
- "provide a decent standard of living for the unemployed"; and
- "provide everyone with a guaranteed basic income."

(The table gives the average of responses favoring government activism on these five "welfarist" issues.)

Hungary	79
West Germany	76
Britain	64
Netherlands	60
Australia	42
United States	**38**

SOURCE: Tom W. Smith, "Inequality and Welfare," in *British Social Attitudes: Special International Report*, ed. Roger Jowell, Sharon Witherspoon, and Lindsay Brook (Aldershot: Gower, 1989), 62.

There is no reason to suppose that Americans are less generous or caring than other people; indeed, as Lipset argues,[16] there is evidence that Americans are more likely to give to charity (including churches and synagogues) or to volunteer their time to help good causes than people in other democracies. These poll responses are more plausibly based on a pervasive anti-statism in American political attitudes. Americans are less likely than others to support even government policies than will benefit themselves, such as wearing seat belts. (The table shows the percentage of those who agree and those who strongly agree that the wearing of seat belts should be required by law.)

Australia	92
Austria	82
West Germany	82
Italy	81
Great Britain	80
United States	**49**

SOURCE: *American Enterprise*, March/April 1990, 115.

Americans are also more likely to believe that they are overtaxed, even though they are less heavily taxed than citizens of most democracies. (The table shows the percentage of those who agree that, for persons with middle incomes, taxes are much too high or too high.)

United States	**70**
Australia	64
Italy	62
Netherlands	60
West Germany	52
Switzerland	51
Austria	47
United Kingdom	41

SOURCE: *American Enterprise*, March/April 1990, 114.

Nor is it plausible to suggest, as the example of Germany shows, that the tolerance of inequality in the United States is a reluctant acceptance of the unpleasant but unavoidable costs of economic success. Other democracies, such as Germany, have combined higher levels of equality with affluence. The American tolerance of inequality is more plausibly associated with a liberal tradition that combines a respect for civil liberties with a belief that individuals should be self-reliant.

Yet it is precisely such generalized statements of values that irritate critics of cultural approaches. Mass publics, as a venerable tradition in public opinion research going back to the writings of Philip Converse would stress, cannot be relied on to realize the implications of the general principles to which they think they subscribe. At the least, critics would suggest, we should note that such generalized statements of support for the "American way" coexist with high and stable levels of support for government spending on a variety of programs. As Thomas Ferguson and Joel Rogers argued in rejecting the view that the "Reagan Revolution" reflected an upsurge of conservative public opinion in the late 1970s and 1980s:

> The strength of public support for any given spending initiative is best assessed in the context of other spending priorities. Public perception of trade-offs between military and social outlays [under Reagan] clearly played an important part in diminishing support for the [military] buildup.... Polls over the period between early 1981 and late 1983 showed that support for increased domestic spending grew from 49 percent to 67 percent for programs directed to the poor, from 43 percent to 75 percent for education programs, and from 49 percent to 66 percent for health programs—all while support for military spending declined.[17]

The most complete exploration of public opinion in a critical area for assessing how the "liberal tradition" relates to practical politics is Fay Lomax Cook and Edith J. Barrett's *Support for the American Welfare State*.[18] Cook and Barrett take two essential steps for accurate assessment of public support for the welfare state. First, they distinguish between programs. As they note, although commercial polling organizations typically ask about public attitudes toward "welfare" spending, there is no government program with that title; each respondent must construct his or her own meaning for such questions by deciding which of a range of programs the interviewer has in mind. In fact, the welfare state consists of numerous different programs, some of which (such as Social Security, targeted on the retired) receive very different levels of support from others (such as Aid to Families with Dependent Children). A second crucial step taken by Cook and Barrett is to attempt to make their test of public support for welfare-state programs real by asking respondents in their survey whether they would be prepared to back up generalized support for programs with a commitment such as paying higher taxes. This is an important test to apply because simple questions about whether government programs should be increased, maintained, or cut are often criticized on the grounds that those who feel that "something should be done" about an obvious social problem are prompted to support government action, a step that, given other choices, they might not support.

Cook and Barrett found that even during the years in which the Reagan administration was calling for major cuts in welfare, there was a high level of general support for the welfare state. The most popular programs were, not surprisingly, those from which all expect to benefit one day, such as Medicare and Social Security; only about 3 percent of their sample favored cutting these programs. The least popular, Aid to Families with Dependent Children and Food Stamps, were targeted on the poor; 16 percent and 24 percent of the sample respectively wanted to cut these programs. Similarly, a large proportion of Cook and Barrett's sample was content to pay taxes to support a variety of social welfare policies. While, as might be expected, more people were content to pay taxes to support Social Security (81 percent) than AFDC (65 percent), the degree to which the public was prepared to fund AFDC is the more surprising finding. Nevertheless, whereas a high proportion (58 percent) of the public is prepared to pay more taxes to avoid cuts in Social Security or to engage in political activity such as letter writing in support of that program, only about 36 percent of the public claim to be prepared to pay more in taxes or write letters in defense of AFDC.[19] Cook and Barrett provide an emphatic answer to the question of how widespread support is for the American welfare state.

> After more than fifty years of expansion, the American welfare state faced a serious threat in the 1980s when the Reagan administration proposed a dramatic scaling back of the federal role in financing pro-

grams. Although the Reagan administration did not succeed in all its attempts, it did prompt many American citizens to rethink their support for social welfare. After a watershed decade of questioning the direction of the welfare state, the answer is clear. The public ... supports the social welfare state. [It] does not want any more cuts in the fabric of protection provided to all citizens by social welfare programs. Thus, it appears that the American welfare state is here to stay.[20]

Supporters of the welfare state will note that this conclusion was partly premature. The upsurge of conservative Republicanism culminating in the capture of the House of Representatives and Senate in 1994 called the future of the American welfare state into question once more, two years after Cook and Barrett's book was published. The "welfare reform" legislation (the Personal Responsibility and Work Opportunity Reconciliation Act of 1996) passed by the Republican Congress and signed into law by President Clinton ended the basic program targeted on the neediest, Aid to Families with Dependent Children, and with it the idea originating during the New Deal that there should be a federal guarantee against slipping into deep poverty. Clinton signed the bill into law fearing that otherwise the Republicans would criticize him as "soft on welfare." Moreover, politicians who wish to cut social welfare programs can do so not by criticizing them in principle but by suggesting that the programs are burdened by waste and inefficiency, sentiments with which many Americans are likely to agree whatever the merits of the case. During election campaigns, conservative politicians oblige citizens who want to vote against spending on social programs by reciting numerous reasons why they are not really voting against the poor and needy. Yet while Cook and Barrett's assessment of popular support for the welfare state might seem too high, it is at least a convincing refutation of the idea that Americans are simply liberal individualists unwilling to support a welfare state. When we shift discussion away from generalizations about "welfare" and onto specific government programs, a large proportion of Americans are supportive, even if it means paying more in taxes. When President Clinton argued in the late 1990s that emerging budget surpluses should be devoted to protecting Social Security rather than reducing taxes, he was taking a popular position.

The dominance of the "liberal tradition" has often been invoked to explain the weakness of organized labor in the United States, even though there have been periods in American history (such as the early 1950s) when unions in the United States recruited as high a proportion of workers as did unions in Britain. Because liberalism stresses individual effort and achievement, not collective action, we might suppose that if the "liberal tradition" were unchallenged, Americans would be hostile to organized labor and sympathetic to business. Providing reliable evidence on whether this is indeed the case, the periodic American National Election Studies ask respondents to pick a point on a feeling thermometer to illustrate how warmly (favorably) or coldly (unfavorably) they feel toward business and labor; the scale ranges from o (very cold) to 100 (very warm). (The table reports the feeling thermometer score averages in three score ranges, o to 45 degrees, 45 to 55 degrees, and 55 to 100 degrees, over a span of thirty-one years.)

	0–45 degrees		*45–55 degrees*		*55–100 degrees*	
	Business	*Labor unions*	*Business*	*Labor unions*	*Business*	*Labor unions*
1964	13	21	37	29	51	50
1966	13	21	38	27	49	53
1968	14	20	36	33	50	48
1972	25	24	22	21	53	55
1974	34	28	22	19	45	53
1976	35	38	21	22	44	40
1980	29	26	17	19	54	55
1984	26	26	30	22	44	52
1986	n.a.	29	n.a.	16	n.a.	56
1988	23	23	27	22	50	55
1990	n.a.	23	n.a.	19	n.a.	57
1992	25	26	26	21	50	52
1994	22	26	21	21	56	52

SOURCE: Calculated by the author from American National Election Studies surveys.

The impression the results give is that most of the population is quite favorably disposed to both business and labor. A surge of antipathy toward both occurred in the 1970s; it subsided thereafter, though antipathy to business did not return to the very low levels of the early 1960s. An important consequence of this cycle of change was that no longer were there significantly more Americans hostile to labor than to business. In 1964, almost twice as many people felt coldly toward unions as felt coldly toward business; by 1994, the difference was slight. Over the thirty-one-year period, the largest single group of Americans felt warmly toward *both* business and labor, defying the determination of many social scientists to see these positions as mutually contradictory.

One might suppose that people who feel warmly toward business would feel coolly toward labor. In practice, this is not the case. There is a very modest correlation (0.15) between the feeling thermometer scores for business and labor. The correlation is positive, however, not negative, as it would be if those who are antilabor were also probusiness; the existence of this modest association suggests that there is some tendency for those who are well disposed to labor to be well disposed to business also. As Lipset and William Schneider argue,[21] public regard for business and labor suffered in the 1970s along with the general decline in confidence in major institutions in the United States, including government. Hostility to unions focuses on them as organizations, not as working people; whereas a majority of the public thinks that unions have too much power, it also thinks that working people have too little.[22] Similarly, criticism of business focuses on antagonism not to capitalism as such but to the alleged dangers of the concentration of power in the hands of large corporations. "Bigness," not business, is the problem, as are the misdeeds of union leaders, not unions as such.[23]

The most striking aspect of public opinion, however, is that it shows such little generalized hostility to labor. Except for rare and puzzling upsurges of antiunion sentiment (as in 1976, which coincided with an upsurge of antibusiness sentiment), only a small minority of the population can be described as antiunion. In the period between 1964 and 1994, less than one quarter (24 percent) on average of the public was "cold" (0–45 degrees) on the feeling thermometer toward unions, a figure indistinguishable from the average for business (24 percent).

Civil Liberties

As Lipset has reminded us, the constituent elements of the American ideology usually have more than one side.[24] The individualism that prescribes a modest role for government in helping people in need, often seen by foreigners as callous indifference to suffering, is also associated with the commitments to freedom, often seen as one of the most attractive features of the American polity. Americans proclaim a strong attachment to their Constitution, including commitments to liberties enshrined in the Bill of Rights such as freedom of speech, assembly, religion, and the press. Somewhat to the irritation of foreigners who think that they, too, subscribe to these beliefs (the French and British imagine their ancestors played an important part in developing them), these liberties are often thought of in the United States as distinctly American.

The belief that Americans are unusually strongly committed to democratic freedoms runs into several difficulties, however.

The first difficulty is whether the general support for the Bill of Rights is a statement of patriotic (or nationalistic) loyalty to one of the founding documents of the nation, rather than to the principles it contains. Just as hostility to "government handouts" in principle coexists with support for Social Security in practice, so support for civil liberties in the abstract has coexisted with persecution of unpopular people. Famous examples of intolerance in comparatively recent American history (the Palmer Raids after World War I harassing leftists, McCarthyism and its attacks on so-called communists after World War II, the "speech code" movements on campuses in the 1980s and 1990s) are all reminders that Americans have not always honored in practice the principles of the Bill of Rights. A vast literature has developed on the degree to which Americans are genuinely committed to the democratic value of tolerating views with which they disagree. This literature initially demonstrated that Americans' willingness to tolerate someone with unpopular views, such as a communist speaking in their neighborhood, was limited. Some researchers argued subsequently that survey data suggested that there had been an increase in tolerance in the mass public. Others contended that the apparent upsurge of tolerance in reality reflected merely a reduced fear of communism; if given the opportunity to choose a group that they particularly disliked and then decide whether they would allow its members to exercise basic democratic rights such as freedom of speech, Americans continued to display high levels of intolerance.[25]

A second difficulty arises with the view that Americans are more committed to abstract freedoms than citizens of other countries. Peter

Taylor-Gooby presents data suggesting that support in the United States for several democratic rights is not unusually high. The accompanying table shows the percentage of respondents saying that the items listed in the left column should "definitely" or "probably" be allowed:

	Australia	West Germany	Italy	Britain	United States
Protest meetings	91	91	79	89	78
Protest pamphlets	87	73	79	86	69
Marches/demonstrations	69	31	67	70	66
Nationwide strike	22	42	59	30	20

SOURCE: Peter Taylor-Gooby, "The Role of the State," in *British Social Attitudes: Special International Report,* ed. Roger Jowell, Sharon Witherspoon, and Lindsay Brook (Aldershot: Gower, 1989), 46.

Similarly, in "hard cases" in which liberties had to be set against competing values, Americans were not distinctive. The table shows the percentage of respondents agreeing with the statements listed in the left column:

	Australia	West Germany	Italy	Britain	United States
Conscience should come before breaking law	68	88	60	61	56
Newspapers should be allowed to publish confidential					
defense plans	16	23	24	26	17
economic news	60	63	64	63	61

SOURCE: Taylor-Gooby, "Role of the State," 47.

Of course, Europeans and Australians may be as likely as Americans to proclaim a commitment to general principles that in practice they would be unwilling to apply to unpopular minorities. Taylor-Gooby made a limited approach to this problem by asking whether people would allow revolutionaries ("people who want to overthrow the government by revolution") and racists ("people who believe that whites are superior to all other races") to enjoy civil liberties or hold certain jobs; the table shows the percentage of respondents answering affirmatively (either "definitely" or "probably"):

	Austra-lia	West Germany	Italy	Britain	United States
Would allow revolu-tionaries					
to hold meetings	51	77	42	54	55
to teach 15-year-olds in school	13	19	20	13	21
to publish books ex-pressing their views	61	74	53	68	57
Would allow racists					
to hold meetings	39	50	28	40	59
to teach 15-year-olds in school	11	16	17	13	24
to publish books ex-pressing their views	47	53	39	53	58

SOURCE: From Taylor-Gooby, "Role of the State," tables 3.2 and 3.3.

Americans are more likely to allow civil liberties to racists than are citizens of the other countries in Taylor-Gooby's study. Americans are much the same as others in their tolerance of revolutionaries, however. While small differences may exist here and there in willingness to extend civil liberties to these groups, the overall impression is that Americans are not exceptional.

The Crucial Importance or the Irrelevance of Culture?

We noted earlier Richard Hofstadter's celebrated dictum that it was the fate of Americans not to have an ideology but to be one.[26] American national identity has been defined neither by blood or race, nor by long-standing identification with a landscape or a culture, but by adherence to the principles of the liberal tradition. As we have seen, these principles command considerable support at the general or theoretical level. It is much less clear, however, what the impact of these principles is in practice. Contemporary scholars are much less willing than was Hartz to accept that American politics has ever been dominated by an ideological consensus; within a very general liberal framework, contending ideas and beliefs about politics and policy have been at play. Moreover, how competing claims from the liberal tradition such as justice and freedom are resolved in terms of practical politics cannot be determined in the abstract. Finally, there is substantial evidence, as we have seen, that ordinary citizens adopt policy positions that conflict substantially with principles from the liberal tradition that they claim to support. Americans subscribe to the "liberal tradition" in the abstract, but not necessarily when it comes to discussing specific policies or problems.

Does all of this mean that the apparently powerful liberal tradition in America is in fact irrelevant? Such an argument carries skepticism too far. The principles of the liberal tradition constitute a source of legitimate ideas and sanctified principles to which politicians can appeal. Opinion polls show a tremendously high level of support for principles embodied in the Bill of Rights, so long as people are aware that it is the Bill of Rights they are discussing. Scholars have shown that while the general principle that all should be able to state their views freely is widely accepted, most Americans would try to prevent members of unpopular groups from enjoying free speech. Yet the fact that free speech is widely accepted in principle provides members of unpopular groups with a powerful weapon. An unpopular group may not always have its rights respected, but it is more likely to have those rights respected if it can point to widely held general principles (freedom of speech, freedom of assembly) than if such rights were not generally accepted. Similarly, interest groups or politicians who wish to oppose government policies such as gun control or environmental regulation stand a better chance than they otherwise would because the liberal tradition supports a general tendency to oppose government domination, "interference," or power. In a society that has long been trained in suspicion of government power (and less trained in fear of the power of business corporations), attacks on "government bureaucrats" have a better chance of success, whatever their motives.

Arguments that the distinctive political culture of the United States does not shape its public policy invite another question. Is it merely coincidence that, as the liberal tradition would require, government in the United States has been somewhat smaller and less likely to adopt welfare state programs than governments in most democracies? The almost total absence of government ownership of industries in the

United States seems to have been prefigurative now that countries such as Britain are privatizing government-owned concerns. Yet that absence of government ownership of businesses did indeed manifest a hesitation about extending government involvement in the running of the economy that once set the United States apart from most other democracies. The refusal of the United States to ensure through government action the availability of health care for all also appears to suggest that Hartz's arguments have continuing validity. Those who reject cultural explanations for America's exceptionalism are under some obligation to provide a better alternative.

One recurring idea has been that the distinctiveness of American policy is a consequence of the distinctive institutions of the United States. Perhaps our political institutions do not reflect our views accurately? At one time it was supposed that factors such as the seniority system in Congress gave conservatives disproportionate power, an argument that Anthony King refuted convincingly even before the seniority system and its results changed.[27] A more plausible idea is that our institutions frame the choices in a distorting manner. Sven Steinmo has recently offered an interesting institutional explanation for policy choices such as the government's decision not to ensure the availability of health care.[28] Steinmo argues that the separation in American institutions of responsibility for taxing from responsibility for spending results in a chronic shortage of revenue. Decisions about how much to tax, never popular in any democracy, are separated from decisions about what to spend, always a more popular question. Taxation is handled by one set of congressional committees, for example, and spending by another. In parliamentary systems, the linkage between spending and taxing is clear. Are such institutional explanations more convincing than those set in the shifting sands of culture and political beliefs? In practice, institutions, too, change and yield when there is sufficient political will. When the United States has set its mind on a goal (winning World War II, putting a man on the moon), it has found the revenue to do so. The culturalists' contention that the United States lacks the political will to provide national health insurance is more convincing than suggestions that institutions get in the way.

Perhaps the most plausible conclusion is that, to borrow Ellis's phrase, American political culture has been a prism, not a prison. General notions about the appropriate role of government have had a limited impact on support for specific policies. The individualistic political traditions of the United States have neither prevented the expansion of government nor guaranteed support for democratic practices such as free speech for unpopular groups. Yet it would be a brave—or foolhardy—analyst who wanted to ignore culture totally.

Yet just as culture seems more relevant than some political scientists would like to admit, it is less determining than others have contended. As we see in chapter 4, the liberal tradition, supposedly confining the size and role of government in the United States, in practice has failed during the twentieth century to prevent a dramatic expansion of American government. In using American political traditions to explain relatively small contrasts between the United States and other advanced industrialized countries, we must be careful not to ignore the fact that these traditions failed to block a radical change during the twentieth century in the size and scope of the American state.

3

The Content
of American Politics

UPPOSE, AS according to supermarket tabloids happens regularly, you have been picked up by aliens from another planet and taken into their spacecraft. Familiar with the concept of politics from experience on their home planet and in their galactic federation, the aliens ask what American politics is about. They emphasize that their question is not about the familiar topics of political science courses such as parties, elections, courts, Congress, and the presidency, which together make up the *structure* of our political system, but about the *content* of our politics. What do we—and our politicians—spend our time discussing and disputing when we talk politics? What do we believe are the major issues that our politicians should be addressing, and what issues do our politicians devote their energies to?

As you struggle to produce a coherent answer to this question in the unfamiliar setting of an alien spacecraft, a host of political issues tumble into your mind, such as the management of the economy, poverty, race relations, crime, the environment, women's rights, defense, and foreign policy. To your relief, the visiting aliens are satisfied with your answers to their original question, but they follow it with two others. Has the content of our politics changed much, the aliens ask, and is there anything distinctive about *American* politics compared to the politics of other earthly countries they have overflown? Are we still focused on the same issues today that occupied our attention ten, twenty, forty, or fifty years ago; is our politics concerned with the same issues that dominate the politics of other advanced democracies?

There are at least four common perspectives on the contents of our politics. One of them suggests that we shall find little of interest to study. Politics is now and always has been about the pursuit of material interests through macro- and microeconomic policies. I term this view (explored further below) "bluff realism." A second and by now familiar perspective on American politics is that it is "exceptional"; not only the institutional forms of American politics but the actual content of American politics differ from those in other democracies. Americans have distinctive political concerns and, as premised by Louis Hartz,[1] are adherents to a "liberal tradition" and so are less inclined to seek to solve economic and social problems through political action. A third and contrary view, which I term "sociological determinism," suggests that capitalist societies are evolving similarly in their politics as in their economies. Again, this argument is developed further below. The fourth and final argument explored in this chapter is the claim that we have witnessed a major change in the content of our politics since the 1960s. The American agenda is changing, moving away from classic concerns about the role and size of government that can be traced back to the Progressive or New Deal era and toward a greater concern with sharply conflicting values or lifestyles; a "new liberalism" confronts a "new conservatism."

Perhaps in response to the well-known criticism of pluralism that control over the political agenda—deciding what is subject to decision—is one of the highest forms of power, political scientists have made the political agenda a crucial research area since the early 1970s.[2] These scholars approach the political agenda in a variety of ways, however. Important studies have examined how individual issues find their way onto the political agenda. Thus the well-known work of John Kingdon[3] and, more recently, that of Frank Baumgartner and Bryan Jones[4] delineate the conditions under which an issue becomes established on the political agenda. A very different approach is concerned not so much with showing how individual issues find their way onto the agenda as with the general character of the political agenda in a particular historical period. This approach is found most commonly in the historically based party literature, where it is common to claim that late-nineteenth-century politics was organized around the tariff[5] or that politics from the 1930s until some uncertain more recent date was about the issues of government involvement in the economy and society that are associated with the New Deal.[6] Here the concern is with categorizing and explaining the substance of the agenda as a whole. This chapter is in the second tradition, although the political agenda, not parties or other political actors, remains its focus.

Bluff Realism

The bluff realist perspective suggests that there is nothing particularly problematic in the content of politics. Citizens and politicians use politics to pursue their selfish interests. Politicians seek to gain or retain office in democracies by offering voters policies that voters believe will advance their material well-being. Politics is dominated by discussion of how to promote full employment and economic growth and by promises of subsidies or regulations that confer benefits ("rents") on groups that are sufficiently organized and numerous to have power in the political system.[7]

Bluff realists expect to find considerable continuity in American politics and much similarity between American politics and the politics of other advanced democracies. Human nature is much the same around the world and over time; each person purposively pursues his or her self-interest in politics as in other aspects of life. Bluff realists point to the apparent importance of economic factors in determining the outcome of elections. In both the United States and Britain, a substantial body of research shows a close connection between the performance of the economy and the outcome of elections.[8] The party holding the White House (or constituting the government in Britain) can expect to be rewarded if economic variables such as employment and growth levels are favorable, and it can expect to be punished if such variables worsen.

Political folklore also celebrates the importance of "lunch pail" issues. In one of the most famous moments in the 1980 campaign, in which Ronald Reagan became the first presidential candidate in this century to defeat a Democratic incumbent, Reagan asked citizens to "ask yourself whether you are better off now than you were four years ago." In 1992, when Governor Bill Clinton, emphasizing economic improvements, defeated a Republican president who had enjoyed record popularity following his triumph in the Gulf War, Clinton's campaign headquarters was said (not quite accurately) to be festooned with a banner reading "It's the economy, stupid!"[9] Appeals to citizens based generally on their self-interest can be supplemented by promises of subsidies to groups, which may find some way to exert political leverage, thus becoming one of the subgovernments that Theodore Lowi[10] asserts to be characteristic of the second American republic. A group that can claim plausibly to hold the balance of power in an election campaign is in a particularly fortunate position, of course. Groups such as farmers and the elderly have been the recipients of large-scale government support because they can claim that their votes are sufficiently numerous to determine the outcome of election campaigns.

Bluff realism has the appeal of sounding like hard-headed common sense. Yet it fails to comprehend the complexities of political life. Even in areas where it seems most plausible (such as its claims for the dominance of economic issues), the situation is more complicated than it suggests. Research indicates that individual voters are less influenced by the direct impact of economic trends on them personally than by their evaluations of how the economy is performing in general. Voters are concerned with what appears to be the state of the national lunch pail, rather than just their own.[11]

Bluff realists also run the risk of overlooking important changes in what governments can or should deliver, and hence what politicians can promise. For example, the belief that governments have the ability to control the economy by either fiscal or monetary policy is historically limited. Before the Keynesian revolution in economics, few would have thought that government had the ability to ameliorate adverse trends in the economic cycle; powerful critiques of Keynesianism may have already ended the era in which expectations are that governments have the capacity to deliver prosperity.

Recent developments in American politics have also reminded us that entrepreneurial politicians can benefit from attacking the benefits accorded groups (the poor, scholars in the humanities and social sciences) that are seen as illegitimate by large sections of the electorate. If subjected to popular attacks, the subgovernments given such prominence by Lowi may crumble; subgovernments require a modicum of acceptance to continue. Finally, bluff realism, by stressing continuity, seems insensitive to obvious changes in politics. Under the right conditions, some apparently unlikely issues do seem to find their way onto the political agenda. Women's rights were absent from the political agenda in the 1950s; they have received more attention since. While we commonly make errors such as supposing that prior to the 1970s there was no feminism or prior to the 1960s no concern for civil rights, we must recognize that the prominence of these issues in our politics varies. The content of our politics is less fixed or stable than bluff realists suggest.

America's Exceptionalism

Perhaps the most powerful interpretation of American politics is the exceptionalist perspective discussed in the preceding chapter. Because it already has received extended discussion, there is little point in doing more here than predicting what it would lead us to find on—and off—the American political agenda. In brief, if the liberal tradition perspective is well founded, we should expect to find surprisingly little debate about economic and social issues, few calls for the expansion of the role of government in caring for individual citizens, and, conversely, considerable attention to such core liberal principles as civil liberties, democratic governance, and political reform.

Sociological Determinism

The observation that there are important similarities in the public policies of developed nations is not new. Indeed, a powerful tradition in analyzing the growth of the welfare state has argued that a nation's level of economic development is the most powerful factor in explaining the level of its social welfare expenditure.[12] Whatever developed countries profess politically, their levels and patterns of expenditure look much the same. Debates over the question of how much, if at all, politics matters in determining the level of welfare expenditure tends to give way to analysis of how politics determines the type of welfare state that is created, and in particular the bases on which claims for support can be made. Thus Esping-Anderson contrasts the insurance-based claims of "liberal" welfare states with the citizenship-rights-based claims of Scandinavian welfare states.[13]

We should surely expect to find some relationship between the nature of a society and its politics. It would be odd to find, for example, that railroads attract as much attention today as when they were the primary means of transport. Clearly we would expect the great changes that have occurred in American society since World War II—the move to the suburbs, the growth of white-collar employment, the changed position of women, and the spread of the race issue throughout the nation—to have an impact on the nation's politics.

The relationship between social change and political change is not simple, however. A large body of social science is concerned to show how and why issues do not enter the political agenda. Even Marx in *The Eighteenth Brumaire of Louis Bonaparte* was concerned to show how the practicalities of the lives of French peasants constrained their political influence. Modern social scientists have also advanced numerous reasons why social groups may not be able to place their concerns on the political agenda. Some groups may lack the resources to do so, while others, whose widely dispersed members stand to gain little personally from policy changes (consumers are such a group), may find the problems of collective action hard to overcome. Political institutions are organized in ways that keep the concerns of some interests prominent when they have long passed the peak of their societal importance. Yet the institutional privileging of one interest denies attention to others; the number of concerns that can be fitted onto the political agenda is limited.

Furthermore, the interests and concerns of groups in society do not pass directly onto a ready-formed political agenda. Groups respond not only to their own needs but to perceived opportunities to pursue them. Victoria Hattam argues, for example, that American and British workers faced very different circumstances in the late nineteenth century.[14] The conservative activism of the American judiciary in that period made political activity less rewarding, for even if successful politically, workers might find their gains annulled by judicial *diktat*. The ease with which loosely structured parties in the United States can be influenced by movements has been a powerful disincentive to creating new parties. Yet the means by which a group pursues its objectives has an important, reciprocal impact on its understanding of its interests. If a group channels its efforts through a political party, it will be under significant pressures both to broaden its concerns to include interests previously ignored and simultaneously to avoid "extreme" positions on its own interests that might cost the party electoral support. In short, the political process of pursuing an interest affects the way in which that interest is defined or operationalized.

We should also note that social scientists and historians have often seen political issues as a way of compensating for, not addressing, social change. Thus Richard Hofstadter suggested that the rise of Progressivism and Prohibition were the results of status anxiety.[15] Established local elites, frightened by social trends such as urbanization and large-scale immigration, took emotional refuge in campaigning for issues that did little to resolve their real problems but did give them emotional release. Prohibition did not return a single immigrant to Italy or save a single family farm; it did, however, assert the supremacy of traditional values.

Few political scientists today would suggest that social forces create political issues directly, however. Political institutions, including parties, facilitate or inhibit the passage of different types of issues onto the political agenda. Whether social change is followed by creation of a new issue is a matter for investigation, not assumption.

New Politics Perspectives

A final perspective on the political agenda would lead us to expect considerable change in the content of American politics. This perspective suggests that there has been a permanent shift in the nature of political issues that preoccupy Americans. Whereas the old politics, exemplified by the New Deal issues, was concerned with helping us find the means by which to live and work, the new politics is concerned with issues about how, and how well, we live. Such issues may be concerned with political ideals, such as participation, or with the ways in which we treat or mistreat the earth. "New politics" emerged from the upheavals of the late 1960s and early 1970s; many of its leaders may have been drawn into politics by their opposition to the Vietnam War. Such activists often viewed both the politicians and organizations of the Old Left with considerable suspicion; Democratic politicians such as Senator Hubert Humphrey, long associated with the liberal wing of the party, and interest groups such as the AFL-CIO (which had been in the vanguard on issues such as civil rights and Medicare) were seen by new politics activists as exemplifying the old, corrupt order.

The most complete academic research arguing that a new politics orientation existed among the mass public was Ronald Inglehart's.[16] Drawing on Maslow's argument that humans have a hierarchy of needs, Inglehart suggested that as our standard of living rises, we have focused less on material issues and more on issues concerned with values and lifestyles. Inglehart's work helped explain the rise of new social movements in Europe and the United States, movements advancing "postmaterialist" concerns, such as the protection of the environment. The long period of affluence in both Europe and the United States ultimately produced not apolitical contentment but new social movements pressing for a transformation of society to achieve new, nonmaterialist objectives.

There are several obvious problems with the new politics perspective, however. The first is whether there actually are "new" political issues involved. Many of the issues pressed by the New Left in the United States in the 1970s were actually not so new. Protection of the environment had been a concern in the United States early in the twentieth century, even though the character of environmentalism might have changed in the intervening decades. Interestingly, other issues of the 1970s, such as increasing opportunities for participation in political parties through primaries, women's rights, and consumer protection had also been prominent on the political agenda in that period, generally known as the Progressive era. We might argue, therefore, that the United States has experienced not the emergence of new politics but a series of reform cycles; the same type of issue that was so prominent in the Progressive era reemerged in the 1960s and 1970s only, reform-cycle authors suggest, to fade thereafter.

A second problem is that much of the new politics writing has focused on the left. The research on new social movements, for example, seems to assume that all of these movements are on the left, distrusting and disliking the consequences of capitalism. In practice, some of the most active social movements in the United States in the 1980s and 1990s have been conservative movements, strongly supportive of capitalism but enraged by the behavior and attitudes of cultural and political elites. Campaigns for allowing school prayer, ending a woman's right to choose to end a pregnancy, or stopping "liberal bias" in the media are not hostile to capitalism or American institutions. Very frequently campaigners see themselves as restoring or maintaining a better world in the face of challenges from a dangerous new order. In short, they are a far cry from the affluent postmaterialists celebrated or criticized for turning on the same free enterprise institutions that give them a high standard of living.

A third problem is that while the newer movements of both the left and the right have remained prominent since the late 1960s, we have learned not to take prosperity for granted. In each of the last three decades of the twentieth century, the United States (and the developed world more generally) has experienced severe economic problems. The oil shocks of the early 1970s, the severe recessions of the early 1980s and early 1990s, and the fact that real wages in the United States have stagnated since the early 1970s have made the state of the economy a topic of great concern. The idea that we have entered a postmaterialist phase in our politics is less convincing today than when the idea was first advanced.

Even if some of the explanations for the rise of new politics are unconvincing, they do draw our attention to the possibility that there has been significant change in the relative importance of different types of issues on the political agenda. We have the impression, at least, that both liberals and conservatives did succeed in placing new issues on the political agenda. From the late 1960s onward, issues such as protecting the environment and consumers, defining abortion rights, and ensuring the rights of women in American society seem to have taken on a significance politically that they did not have before. Indeed, part of the strategy that brought the Republicans such success was to raise the prominence of "wedge issues": abortion, race, and respect for traditional values such as support for the family and patriotism. Republicans hoped that these issues would separate supporters of the Democrats on New Deal issues (such as full employment, Social Security, and workers' rights) from their party. Whether or not we can explain it, we feel that the political agenda has shifted.

Studying the Political Agenda

How can we determine what the political agenda has been at some point in the past? The character of the American political system raises formidable problems. The constitutional system of separated institutions sharing powers, coupled with the fragmentation of those institutions into a highly decentralized system of agencies, committees, and subcommittees, makes it much more difficult to determine the content of *the* political agenda in the United States than in a centralized parliamentary system such as Britain. In its fullest sense the U.S. political agenda is a combination of the agendas of dozens, perhaps hundreds, of different institutions. We do, however, have a clear sense of what the central political issues are at any particular moment.

It is also necessary to recognize that the presence of an issue on the political agenda does not mean that it is of great significance. Issues on the political agenda may not be of enduring importance, and vice versa. The decision to build the atomic bomb was arguably one of the most important decisions of the modern era. Yet it was unknown to the public and could in no way be said to have been prominent on the political agenda at the time. Similarly, the Civil Rights Act of 1964 can be regarded as the legal foundation of current policies attempting to achieve gender equality. Yet little attention was paid to the adoption of legislative language covering gender as well as racial discrimination. In brief, there is no necessary connection between the importance of a topic and its presence on or absence from the political agenda.

The concept of the political agenda adopted here is thus entirely subjective, at least to contemporaneous observers. My test for including a topic on the political agenda of any given year is whether there is evidence that people at the time thought it was important. Again, however, practical problems arise. There is no one person or institution whose enumeration of the issues of the day is decisive (to take a current example, President Clinton, former Senator Dole, and Speaker Gingrich all have different ideas about what the key issues of the day are). Therefore I have used three different sources: *Congressional Quarterly*'s list of "key votes" in Congress published annually in its *Almanac,* the "year in review" stories identifying the most important developments in politics that appear in the *New York Times* in December (or, in an election year, in October), and the State of the Union addresses.

All these sources have their advantages. CQ's status as an authoritative record in the Washington community is well known. Not only is the *New York Times* a preeminent newspaper, but the value of its "year in review" stories has been established in studies such as David Mayhew's analysis of divided government.[17] The State of the Union address is probably the president's best opportunity to shape the political agenda for the year, a speech that is guaranteed attention in Washington and indeed in the nation as a whole. In all cases

I measured the prominence of a policy area by calculating what percentage of all the items in its category that it accounted for. Thus, in the easiest case, the figure derived from the *CQ* list is the percentage of the annual total number of "key votes" that were on measures in the policy area in question. The figure for the *New York Times* is the percentage of the total number of crucial issues it identified for the preceding twelve (or nine) months that were part of this policy area. The State of the Union speeches were the most difficult to code because presidents frequently make rhetorical flourishes without policy content. I attempted to code only presidential comments that announced or called for some form of action such as deployment of troops, passage of a law, the promulgation of regulations, and the like. This was intended to avoid counting references to amber waves of grain or fruited plains as a reference to agricultural policy.

The categories used are more or less self-explanatory. "Government" refers to proposals for reform or debates about standards and values in government. "Crime and guns" encompasses issues such as gun control, the death penalty, and criminal procedure. "Health and education" covers the involvement of the federal government in aiding education or in providing national health insurance; "housing and poverty" refers to proposals for federal support for low-income housing or aid to the poor. "Energy and the environment" covers proposals to protect the environment or encourage energy conservation. "Civil rights" and "immigration" are self-explanatory; "women and abortion" covers the rights of women, including that fundamental but controversial issue, reproductive control. "Foreign policy and defense" covers both general policy and acquisitions decisions that in practice cannot be disentangled from debates about strategy. Similarly, arguments about the level of taxation and government spending were so intertwined that a single category seemed appropriate. Aid to specific regions, industries, and public works seemed to group together as examples of classic distributive (to borrow Lowi's terminology) policies. "Employment policy" refers to federal regulation of the rights of workers and employers; the Taft-Hartley Labor Act is a classic example. "Economic and trade policy" refers to debates about the management of the economy or policy on issues such as tariffs or trade management.

My purpose here is not to show how individual policy areas have developed, however, but to discover whether broad categories of policy have changed in prominence. I created four groupings of policy types (listed in table 3.1). The first consists of the topics that a bluff realist might see as constituting the core of politics: taxes and levels of government expenditure, aid to specific regions or industries (classic pork-barrel or distributive politics), and debates about economic or trade policy. The second includes a group of issues that exemplify the New Deal vision of the state, a combination of social insurance and some assistance to the needy. This group consists of debates over proposals for federal involvement in providing or funding health care, education, low-income housing, and assistance to the poor; it also contains legislation on the relative power of workers and employers, a policy area (employment) that is clearly distinct intellectually but historically was a core part of the New Deal agenda. The third group consists of the new politics or lifestyle issues that came to prominence

TABLE 3.1

FOUR BROAD CATEGORIES OF POLICY AREAS

Type	Component policy areas
Category I	*The economy and lunch pail issues*
	Economic and trade policy
	Aid to specific regions, industries, public works
	Taxation and government spending
Category II	*The New Deal tradition and government*
	guarantees for citizens
	Health and education
	Housing and poverty
	Employment policy
Category III	*New Politics issues*
	Crime and guns
	Energy and the environment
	Civil rights
	Women and abortion
	Government, reform, standards
Category IV	*Foreign policy and defense*
	Foreign policy
	Defense
	Immigration

in the 1960s and 1970s: civil rights, women's rights (including abortion rights), environmental protection and energy conservation, and crime (including gun control). Again, I do not claim that these issues are linked logically. I believe, however, that they are very much the issues that people have in mind when they say that a post–New Deal agenda has come to dominate American politics. A fourth and final grouping contains two issues that have been of concern to the republic from its earliest days: foreign and defense policy and immigration policy.

Findings

Has any one set of issues dominated American politics since World War II? The different data sources give somewhat different rankings, but as table 3.2 (p. 54) shows, there is considerable overlap among them. Foreign and defense policy emerges as one of the major components of the national political agenda, ranking first or second throughout the period as a whole according to all the data sources. On one hand, this is unsurprising given the dominant international role of the United States. On the other hand, it might be unexpected, given the folklore that the public is uninterested in foreign policy and the finding in opinion polls that the public rarely places foreign policy at the top of its agenda. The prominence of federal aid to education and health care belies any argument that these issues have been excluded from the political agenda, even if proposals to expand the federal role have not always succeeded. Similarly, debates over federal assistance to low-income housing and to the poor themselves have been common on the political agenda. Both Congress and the media (the presidency much less so) have been extensively preoccupied with the running of government itself—the standards of people in government, procedural reforms, and so forth. Environmental protection and energy conservation have also figured prominently on the agenda, according to all three data sources.

What is more striking is how little space on the political agenda has been accorded to the new politics issues (other than the environment) that allegedly play such a massive role in our politics. Feminists will not be surprised (though their opponents may be) by the low ranking of women's rights in all the data sources, even after this category was expanded to include an area (abortion) where most of the debate has been dominated by proposals to restrict freedom of choice

TABLE 3.2
RANKING OF ATTENTION GIVEN TO POLICY AREAS
BY DATA SOURCE, 1947–90

	Rank in data source			
Policy area	CQ	NYT	State of the Union	Average
Foreign policy, defense	1	1	2	1
Aid to specific regions, industries, public works	2	6	7	5
Government, reform, standards	3	3	6	3
Health, education	4	2	1	2
Energy, the environment	5	5	4-5	4
Housing, poverty	6	8	4-5	7
Employment policy	7	7	9-10	8
Civil rights	8	11	9-10	10
Taxation, government spending	9	9	8	9
Economic and trade policy	10	4	3	6
Immigration	11	10	13	11
Women, abortion	12	13	12	13
Crime, guns	13	12	11	12

and access to abortion. Immigration (again defined inclusively) has been a minor issue in the period as a whole. Crime and gun control, celebrated as focal points of cultural conflict, have together ranked very low for all data sources.

Certain differences in the rankings in different data sources are clear and understandable. As befits its reputation, Congress (according to CQ) made distributive politics such as aid to specific regions or industries more prominent on its agenda than would have been suggested by the other data sources; Congress also showed a striking tendency to devote less attention to general economic and trade policy than did the media or the president. Presidents, as their claims to speak for more national interests would also suggest, have worried more about general levels of taxation and government spending.

Those who believe that a new liberalism and a new conservatism have come to dominate our politics might reply that no one should expect new politics issues to dominate the political agenda in the entire period since World War II; only since the late 1960s have these issues taken on such importance. Thirteen figures in the appendix display the shifts in the prominence of different policy areas on the political agenda according to each data source.

Several noticeable trends are suggested by these figures. The distributive politics of aid to specific industries or regions has retained significance on the political agenda but is less important than it once was. In an important interpretation of American politics, Richard Franklin Bensel argued that "regional competition has been fundamental with the American political system."[18] While this may well have been true in the past, it does not seem that regional competition is as important today. Another area becoming less prominent on the political agenda is labor law. Disputes about the rights of employers and workers return as an important policy area from time to time but are less significant than they once were. Rather oddly, given concern about the relative performance of the American economy, the prominence of economic and trade policy seems to have declined. Standards in government and procedural reform of government, like crime and gun control, become prominent from time to time, only to fade again. The federal role both in health care and education and in assistance to the poor fluctuates sharply, with some evidence of a decline since the mid-1960s. Civil rights, as we might have predicted, achieved prominence in the late 1950s to mid-1960s, only to fade. The attention given to women's rights (including abortion rights) grew sharply late in the period; whether this is (like civil rights) a spike that will be followed by decline or a trend that will be more enduring remains to be seen. Foreign and defense policy retained almost constant significance, while the attention paid to general levels of taxation and government expenditure increased.

Trends in the prominence of such a large number of policies tend to obscure changes in the political agenda as a whole, however. For the sake of simplicity, the results for all the policy areas in each data source were added together to create a single scale. The results are displayed in figure 3.1 (p. 56).

What picture emerges? The most obvious feature of the figure is that the relative importance of categories on the political agenda fluctuates considerably. Rights and quality-of-life issues (Category III in

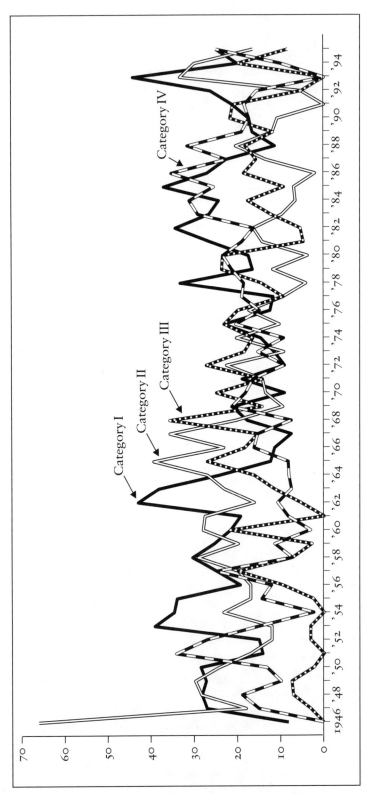

FIGURE 3.1. ISSUE POLICY AREAS, ALL SOURCES COMBINED

SOURCES: CQ key votes; *New York Times*; State of the Union addresses.

table 3.1) were relatively unimportant in the late 1940s but of considerable significance in the late 1960s. Social welfare policy (Category II in table 3.1) dominated the agenda in 1946 and remained an important policy area in 1965; it had declined almost to insignificance in 1986.

The importance of social welfare policy issues overall suggests a second obvious point. The United States may well be exceptional in the comparatively small scale of its welfare state, but the attention that social welfare issues have received in isolated periods suggests that neither American culture nor American institutions have excluded attention to these concerns from the political agenda. The strongest claim associated with culturalists such as Hartz—that American culture cannot support attention to social welfare issues raised by social democrats in other nations—seems to be ill founded. Far from precluding a discussion of these themes, American culture frequently has ceded to them a major portion of the political agenda. Both categories (II and III) that contain proposals for reform, however, show significant "spikes"; as is commonly argued, reformers have been able to stimulate great bursts of attention to both social policy and environmental reforms but have been less able to sustain interest in them.

The high average score for defense and foreign policy (Category IV in table 3.1) in the period since World War II, discussed earlier, represents not dominance in several periods but unusually steady significance on the political agenda. As befits the world's strongest nation, foreign and defense issues are rarely insignificant. The crucial question, however, is whether there has indeed been any clear tendency for the political agenda to be transformed. It seems not. The economic concerns (Category I in table 3.1) that bluff realists see as the core of politics have clearly claimed a conspicuous place on the political agenda since World War II. The decline in the prominence of these issues in the 1960s and early 1970s had been reversed by the early 1990s. Clearly, there is no evidence here to support a postmaterialist view that economic issues have receded in significance. Social welfare proposals were clearly less prominent on the agenda in the 1980s than for much of the period up to 1968. Yet the suspicion that such issues had been displaced by attention to policies within the rights and quality-of-life category seems unfounded. While social welfare policies played a minor role—at times a very minor role—on the political agenda in the 1980s, rights and quality-of-life issues scarcely fared better. A more accurate assessment would be that, between the mid-1970s and the mid-1990s, social welfare issues lost the prominence they had enjoyed on the political agenda in previous decades, while rights and quality-of-life issues no longer commanded the attention they had generated briefly between 1966 and 1972.

Conclusions

The beliefs that the content of American politics is exceptional and that it is radically different today than in the past are widely held. Yet it is far from clear that they are well founded.

A rigorous analysis of the degree to which the American political agenda matches or diverges from the political agendas of other democracies would require a major international project to replicate the procedure we have followed here in assessing the politics of the United States. It is obvious even from the American data, however, that the strongest claims about the distinctiveness of American politics are false. Foreigners observing American politics should not be surprised by the issues that are prominent. Economic and social policy questions pervade the political agenda, as they do in other advanced industrial democracies. Any idea that the "liberal tradition" blocks discussion of such issues is clearly false. It is probable that one area does stand out more prominently on the American political agenda than on the agendas of other democracies: defense and foreign policy. If so, the most obvious explanation would be not American ideology but American power; Americans discuss foreign policy more because, as citizens of the sole surviving superpower, their nation can do more.

The evidence presented in this chapter does allow us to address the questions of whether the American political agenda has changed during the postwar period, and if so, how. While it is clear that the content of the American political agenda has changed, it is less clear that it has changed in the ways claimed by those who argue that we have moved to a new, postmaterialist politics based on conflicts over values. In particular, the decline in the past twenty years in the attention paid to social policy concerns that embodied the New Deal tradition came about not as a result of increased attention to rights and quality-of-life issues but as part of a trend to pay less attention to both of these policies.

The advice that might be given to liberals of different types on the basis of this analysis is clear. Their problems since the 1960s reflect not the triumph of one variant of liberalism (e.g., environmentalism) over another (e.g., concern about social deprivation) but a conservative trend in the late 1970s and 1980s that was to the disadvantage of both. Perhaps the most fundamental question is what has caused the trends described in this chapter in the prominence of different types of policies. That question requires lengthy and separate attention. Having a more complete picture of the trends that have existed in the content of our politics allows us to begin to address that question.

4

The Size of Government

OW BIG IS government in America? The question invites a further query: how do we measure the size of government? One measure would be the number of people who work for government. According to this measure, the size of the federal government in the United States has been relatively stable for some time and in recent years has declined, even though the total population of the United States has risen. Federal civilian employment reached a peak of nearly 3.4 million people during World War II, fell to 2 million in 1947, and then rose, fluctuating between 2.8 and 3 million between 1968 and 1984. Federal employment reached it highest level, 3.1 million, in 1987 and has since declined to under 3 million.[1]

Yet this measure is clearly an inadequate guide to the reach of government because the federal government has always contracted with other governments such as those of states, cities, and counties and with nongovernmental agencies for the supply of goods and services. One federal employee signing checks may be responsible for the employment of thousands at other levels of government or in the private sector. Governments have long bought equipment such as warships and bombers from corporations that are in legal terms separate entities in the private sector. More recently, governments around the world have shown increased readiness to purchase services ranging from the cleaning of their offices to incarcerating criminals from private-sector companies.[2] Counting the number of government employees does not therefore tell us very much about the proportion of the economy controlled by government.

The most basic measure of the size and scope of government in popular use is the proportion of national income controlled by government; gross domestic product (GDP) is the term I have preferred to use here, although the term gross national product (GNP) may be used almost interchangeably. The word *controlled* is used here deliberately in place of the more usual word *spent* because much government expenditure in all democracies is collected and redistributed by government. Governments are the final consumers of many of the goods and services on which they spend, such as tanks or other weapons purchased for the armed services, but one of the major tasks of the modern state is collecting money from one group of citizens through taxation and transferring it to others (the old, the very poor, the disabled). Examples include retirement pensions (generally known in the United States as Social Security), welfare, and disability allowances. Making these transfer payments is one of the most important activities of modern governments, even though the money transferred is finally spent by individuals, not the state. Some of these expenditures, such as Social Security, are made from funds supposedly separated from general government expenditures; many Social Security recipients in the United States imagine erroneously that they are receiving back the money they paid into a sort of government-run savings bank. In fact, Social Security beneficiaries are receiving money raised through taxation and are benefiting from transfer payments, just like welfare recipients.

As is well known, the proportion of GDP controlled by governments in the United States (federal, state, and local) is somewhat smaller than the proportion controlled by governments in other advanced democracies. In the mid-1990s, governments in the United States controlled 35 percent of the GDP, a significantly lower percentage than was controlled by governments in Germany (49 percent), France (52 percent), Italy (53 percent), Britain (44 percent), or Canada (49 percent). Among the advanced industrialized democracies, only Japan had a lower percentage (32 percent).[3] The highest levels of GDP controlled by government were in the Scandinavian countries: Sweden had an exceptionally high proportion in 1992 compared with other countries (67 percent), significantly higher than its neighbor, Norway (57 percent). The share of GDP controlled by government in the United States was therefore below the figure for the Organization for Economic Cooperation and Development (OECD) as a whole (41 percent) and well below the figure for European members of OECD (50 percent of GDP).

The tendency for governments in the United States to control a lower proportion of GDP than is the average for OECD countries as a whole is not a recent or temporary development due to the policies of any one administration.[4] The share of GDP controlled by government does fluctuate as the economy grows or shrinks; a recession will generally increase the proportion as activity in the private sector declines and expenditures by government on programs such as unemployment compensation grow. Thus the percentage of GDP controlled by government in Britain shot up from 37.6 percent in 1989 to 44.1 percent in 1992 largely as a result of a sharp recession. Yet, as table 4.1 shows, the relative position of the United States has changed little.

Indeed, the contrasts between the United States and all OECD nations and between the United States and only European OECD nations deepened during this period, as the proportion of GDP controlled by government remained relatively stable in the United States but increased significantly in Sweden, Italy, and France.

TABLE 4.1

TOTAL GOVERNMENT OUTLAYS AS A PERCENTAGE
OF GROSS DOMESTIC PRODUCT

	1975	1980	1985	1990	1995
Britain	44.4	42.9	44.0	39.9	43.4
Canada	38.5	38.7	45.3	45.9	46.2
France	43.4	46.1	52.1	49.8	53.7
Germany	48.4	47.9	47.0	45.2	49.5
Italy	41.6	41.9	50.9	51.3	51.9
Japan	26.8	32.0	31.6	31.7	35.6
Sweden	48.4	60.1	63.3	59.1	66.2
United States	**34.7**	**33.7**	**36.7**	**33.3**	**33.3**
All OECD nations[a]	36.2	37.3	39.5	39.0	40.8
European OECD nations[a]	43.7	45.4	49.2	47.8	48.7

SOURCE: OECD, *Economic Outlook*, no. 53 (June 1993); idem, no. 59 (June 1996), table A28.

a. Figures for each country are combined using 1987 GDP weights and exchange rates.

The percentage of GDP (or GNP) controlled by government is a better measure of the overall impact of government on a society than the number of people government employs. Yet this statistic is itself an imperfect measure of the extent of government. In assessing whether or not the United States is still "exceptional" in having unusually small government, we might be particularly interested in the degree to which government spends on traditional activities such as providing for the common defense or guaranteeing law and order compared with welfare-state activities such as providing for the old or the poor. Disaggregating government expenditure into its component programs may accentuate America's exceptionalism because of the tendency for European nations and Canada to spend a smaller proportion of GDP on defense and a higher proportion on the welfare state. Government social expenditures as a percentage of GDP tended to be much lower (and to be growing more slowly) in the United States than in other advanced industrialized democracies (see table 4.2).

The fact that the United States lies well behind most other countries in this group that includes Japan but excludes the lavish welfare states (such as Sweden and Norway) suggests that the United States is

TABLE 4.2

SOCIAL EXPENDITURES[a] IN SOME OECD COUNTRIES

	Percentage of GNP		Annual growth of real social expenditure (%)	
	1980	*1990*	*1975–81*	*1981–90*
Britain	18.0	16.9	n.a.	1.8
Canada	17.5	20.2	3.9	4.4
France	24.7	26.7	5.2	3.2
Germany	24.6	22.0	2.3	1.4
Italy	21.2	26.3	n.a.	4.5
Japan	14.3	14.4	6.6	3.9
United States	**13.1**	**12.4**	**1.9**	**2.0**
Average of above countries[b]	19.1	19.9	n.a.	3.0

SOURCE: OECD *Economic Survey: Canada* 1994.

a. Defined as government expenditures on health care, education, pensions, unemployment compensation.
b. Not weighted for size of GNP, etc.

even more exceptional in the level of its social provision than in the total size of its government. The contrast displayed in table 4.2 is all the more remarkable because it includes expenditure on education, a policy area in which the United States has often been thought to be unusually generous. The idea that the United States is exceptional, tied to a tradition of small and limited government, seems to be confirmed.

Yet some special circumstances should be borne in mind. The first is that social expenditures in the United States have been lower in recent years than in Europe because of the greater success of the United States in avoiding high levels of unemployment; whereas in the mid-1990s the rate of unemployment in the United States was about 5 percent, it hovered around 11 or 12 percent in Germany and France. The higher levels of unemployment that Europe experienced in the 1990s had a dual impact on the proportion of GDP devoted to welfare, first by reducing GDP and then by increasing the demand for welfare payments such as unemployment compensation. Second, much of the contrast between the United States and Europe reflects a single policy decision, the refusal in the United States to create national health insurance. Some 13 percent of GDP in the United States is devoted to health care; about one-third of this is covered by government programs such as Medicare and Medicaid. Were the 8 percent of GDP devoted to health care from nongovernmental resources (chiefly private insurance) to be absorbed by government, the contrast between the United States and some European countries with lower levels of government spending (such as Britain) would disappear. The reasons for the failure of attempts such as President Clinton's to introduce national health insurance are therefore extremely important in understanding why government in general in the United States seems smaller than in other countries. We return to this question later.

The most serious objection to using government expenditures as a percentage of GDP as the measure of the size of government, however, is that naturally enough it measures only expenditures. There are more ways than spending by which governments can attempt to achieve their objectives. Tax allowances encourage people to undertake some activities rather than others; for example, granting tax relief on interest paid on home mortgage loans encourages people to buy houses rather than pay rent. Regulations may compel activities that promote social purposes at relatively low cost to government. Indeed, compliance with regulations may cost individuals or corporations considerable sums, while the government's costs for additional inspectors or compliance officers are very small.

As it happens, both of these "off-budget" forms of government programs are particularly common in the United States. The American state, by providing tax incentives and subsidized loans, has been heavily involved in areas often thought of as purely private-sector activities (such as industrial development).

Tax Allowances

The range of tax allowances (also called "tax expenditures") in the United States has been truly impressive. Federal tax allowances for state and local tax payments provide a subsidy to citizens in states such as Wisconsin and New York, which provide above-average levels of social services; citizens in such states can be pleased that their high state taxes will at least offset their federal tax obligations. Donations to charity have been deductible, encouraging contributions to organizations such as universities, churches, and synagogues, as well as the United Way or Red Cross. Taxpayers have also been able to set significant medical expenditures against their federal tax liability, a means whereby government assists them with medical costs.

Economists insist that tax allowances should be regarded in exactly the same light as government spending. Both cost the government money. The loss of revenue for the government due to tax allowances has much the same impact on its budget as additional spending programs. Contrary to popular belief, tax allowances (expenditures) benefit not only the wealthy or corporations, but a wide spectrum of society. Both corporate taxes and personal income taxes incorporate features that government budgeteers consider to be tax expenditures. Investment allowances are as important to corporations as is the right to set home mortgage interest and state income tax payments against federal tax liability to individuals.

Studies of the politics of the tax system show that the purposes of tax allowances are numerous and varied and that they amount to costly tax expenditures. John Witte shows that some of the most expensive tax expenditures are the partial exemption of Social Security payments and the right to set state income tax payments against federal tax liability.[5] Witte also shows, moreover, how costly are the tax allowances given to corporations. In contrast to the tax expenditures that benefit individuals, which have been very stable, tax expenditures for corporations have changed considerably. Cathie Martin has shown that the corporate tax system changes frequently and often radically. In the 1980s alone, Congress adopted three major changes in the tax system, each of which altered the incentives embedded in the tax code. The 1981 tax changes, for example, provided considerable incentives for corporations to invest, thus advantaging most corporations operating in capital-intensive industries. Many of these allowances were revised in 1982. The 1985 tax reforms were intended to be more neutral between different kinds of industries, favoring neither high-tech nor low-tech, labor-intensive nor capital-intensive.[6] Thus the politics of corporate tax allowances sets business against business as well as business against other groups.

The causes of tax allowances are much debated. For some, tax allowances are the consequence of political power: tax "breaks" purchased through political-action-committee contributions or, as Jeffrey Birnbaum describes,[7] the fruits of adroit lobbying. Martin suggests that such a view is simplistic.[8] Tax allowances are the product of coalitions forged between societal forces such as particular industrial sectors and government officials or politicians and designed to pursue policy goals such as growth, not just to pay off supporters. Interests find allies in politics by persuading them that helping the interest group serves the public good.

Whether these policies are wise or whether they are effectively pursued through tax allowances need not detain us here. The crucial point is that a wide variety of economic and social goals are pursued through the tax system, a form of government action that is not reflected in the standard measures of the scale of government, the percentage of GDP or GNP controlled by government. If we accept the economists' argument that tax expenditures are equivalent to actual expenditures, then government in the United States is larger than is commonly thought. Witte estimates that by the early 1980s, tax expenditures were worth $253,515 million.[9] Sven Steinmo cites a similar figure for the early 1980s but sees a continuation of growth in the value of tax expenditures evident in Witte's calculations; by 1986, Steinmo calculates, tax expenditures were worth $424,700 million.[10] This huge sum was equivalent to 10 percent of GDP, or 43 percent of federal expenditures. Allowing for tax expenditures, in short, changes one's view of the size and scope of government in the United States.

Regulation

The United States has had more experience with regulation than any other country. The oldest of the federal regulatory agencies, the Interstate Commerce Commission, was created in 1887, and it survived until 1996. Many of the problems it encountered in regulating the railroads are problems that countries such as Britain are encountering today in regulating utilities such as water, gas, and electricity.

It is difficult to assess what proportion of the American economy has been subject to regulation historically. We can be sure, however, that it is considerable. More or less the entire energy sector (natural gas, oil, and nuclear power) has been subject to regulation of prices and conditions of service at some point in its recent history. All major transport systems (rail, trucking, airlines), telecommunications, television, and radio have been subjected to detailed government controls.

Does Regulation Reflect Government Power?

A vast quantity and variety of literature exists on the politics of the regulation of price and conditions of service, ranging in approach from historical studies to rational-choice perspectives.[11] Across the wide array of methodological approaches, however, there has been a common tendency to argue that regulation has worked to the advantage of the industry being regulated. In some accounts, the problem has been presented as one of "capture." Regulatory agencies began with the commitment to protect the public from exploitation by monopolistic industries. In time, however, practical problems would drive the regulators toward a more collaborative approach to their industry. Regulators would need the cooperation of the regulated industry to gather information on which to base new controls. As with criminal law, regulations work effectively only if they are complied with voluntarily for the most part; it is inconceivable that inspectorates would ever be large enough to be effective by detecting breaches of regulations and imposing sanctions alone. A cooperative rather than confrontational attitude toward the regulated industry would secure better results.

Other perspectives on regulation have emphasized the probability of major imbalances in political power between proponents and opponents of stricter regulation. Proponents of stricter regulation may, if anything, reduce their political efforts once a regulatory agency whose creation they have sought has been established, believing that their problems are over. The regulated industry, in contrast, is likely to redouble its political efforts, only too aware of the potential regulations' threat to profits.

Rational-choice theorists have made a different argument, anticipated (though they generally seemed unaware of the fact) by revisionist historians. Regulation is seen as intended from the outset to advance the interests of the regulated, not the general public. The Civil Aeronautics Board, to take one of the most plausible examples of this perspective, was from the beginning intended not to hold down airline fares but to promote the prosperity and development of the airlines. Historians have reinterpreted the creation of the Interstate Commerce Commission in 1887 as a move by railroads to stabilize a very competitive industry, contrary to the conventional interpretation that portrayed the ICC as the fruit of agitation by farmers in the Grange movement against exploitation by railroads. In the new interpretation, the ICC was created to set freight rates at a higher level than would have been the case in an unregulated market, not to lower rates below the level set by monopolistic railroads. Similarly, though relying on a rational-choice rather than a historical approach, George J. Stigler interprets the licensing of tradesmen such as barbers not as a means of protecting the public but as a means of raising incomes by restricting entry into the trade.[12]

Thus, while it may be widely agreed that regulation has been extensive, there is less agreement that it represents an effective use of state power to alter the behavior of capitalist markets. Regulation may be evidence not of the willingness of Americans to depart from the free market but of the ability of private interests to appropriate state power for their own advantage. The extent of regulation seems less important than its ineffectiveness.

The revisionist and rational-choice perspectives on regulation have themselves been subject to revision. The Interstate Commerce Commission is perhaps the most thoroughly researched example. While it might have been naïve to interpret the creation of the ICC simply as a response to popular criticism of the railroads, it was also simplistic to ascribe its creation to the machinations of the railroads themselves. As is so often the case in American politics, the creation of the ICC—and probably its policies—was the result of complex coalitions of interests. Thus the ICC worked to the advantage of the railroads in reducing competition on long-haul routes such as Chicago to New York, where several railroads competed for business, but it served the interests of small businesses and farmers dependent on a single railroad in areas where there was no competition.

Similarly, the extensive American experience of regulating utilities offers many examples of practices forced on utilities by regulators that advantaged interests other than the stockholders'. American energy utilities are commonly obliged by regulators to maintain service in winter months to customers who have failed to pay their bills, and, even more remarkably, have been required to promote conservation, in a sense reducing demand for their product.

The creation in the 1960s of Medicare and Medicaid was paralleled by the extension of regulation and the development of a more aggressive mode of regulation. The adoption of federal legislation requiring high standards of environmental protection for air, water, and the workplace extended dramatically the reach of federal regulations. The new agencies established to create and enforce regulations in these areas, particularly the Environmental Protection Agency (EPA) and Occupational Safety and Health Administration (OSHA), made the federal government a presence in the daily lives of nearly all businesses. After the creation of the EPA and OSHA, it was plausible to view the entire manufacturing sector as regulated significantly by the federal government.

The new regulatory agencies speedily acquired a reputation for being very different in character from the image of supposedly captured regulated agencies. Whereas the older regulatory agencies had been portrayed as excessively probusiness, the new regulatory agencies were portrayed as inflexible, almost remorseless in pursuit of their goals, with little regard for the problems of business or even common sense. If the image of the older regulatory agencies such as the Civil Aeronautics Board (CAB) was that they protected business profits at the expense of the consumer, the image of the new regulatory agencies was shaped by stories of OSHA inspectors levying fines on employers for not having toilet seats that conformed to OSHA specifications.

A series of studies suggested that American regulators were less likely to adopt a flexible, common-sense approach to problems than inspectors in countries such as Sweden or Britain, whose political cultures supposedly had less sympathy for capitalism than did that of the United States.[13] The first response of a British or Swedish regulator to a problem in the workplace or the environment was likely to be an attempt to work with the employer to solve the problem; the first response of an American regulator was more likely to be the imposition of a fine. American regulation was more vigorous or aggressive than its counterparts in other democracies in pursuit of values such as protecting the environment against market forces.

While the 1980s witnessed a determined drive by the Reagan and Bush administrations to reduce the stringency of regulations affecting business, most of the relevant regulations and agencies survived into the 1990s; in 1996, Republican representatives such as Scott Klug (Wisconsin) were still denouncing the excesses of OSHA. Business groups argued that stricter regulations in the United States constituted a significant burden for American business in international competition; they attempted to have American trade negotiators force foreign countries to adopt comparable standards in order to raise the costs of America's competitors in world markets. The new regulations clearly constituted a preference for goals such as a clean environment over the goals served by the market.

Scholars have been divided, then, on which interests have been served by regulation. Some have contended that regulation has benefited primarily the regulated, others that it has helped consumers (including other industries). In spite of the onslaught of conservative economists, a strong argument can be made that even some of the old-line regulatory agencies that they criticized the most, such as the CAB, actually benefited consumers and promoted efficiency.[14] Probably the answer has varied from agency and industry to agency and industry. Regulation has been more assertive in periods such as the 1970s than in others, when consumer interests were less organized and effective. Yet whatever interests have benefited the most, regulation has been a considerable deployment of state power, increasing the reach of government far beyond the levels shown in its budget.

Indeed, the expansion of the size and scale of government, as indicated by the proportion of GNP it controls, is paralleled by a considerable growth in the impact of government regulations. More businesses in the United States are affected by federal (or state) regulations today than ever before, and those regulations are probably also imposed with unprecedented vigor. Just as government spending programs have expanded considerably since the New Deal, so federal regulations have expanded considerably since the 1960s. New regulations are proposed and promulgated in the pages of the *Federal Register,* and it has been common to use the number of pages in the *Register* (tallied in table 4.3) to assess the rate of increase in regulation.

During the 1970s, the budgets of federal regulatory agencies grew from about $1.4 billion to over $6 billion,[15] although the difficulties in calculating the total cost of regulation, including the costs of compliance paid by the private sector, were clearly significant. In the late 1970s, Murray Weidenbaum and Robert DeFina put the total costs of federal regulation at $66 billion, equivalent to 4 percent of gross national product.[16] The "Reagan Revolution" aspired to a major reduction in regulation, but it was not achieved. Weidenbaum calculated that after the midpoint of Reagan's first term, the size of social regulatory agencies (covering workplace and consumer safety, the environment, etc.) had been reduced only marginally; whereas the number of employees in such agencies had increased by 584 percent from 1970

TABLE 4.3

INCREASES IN GOVERNMENT REGULATIONS

	Number of pages in the Register
1936	2,599
1940	5,307
1943	17,553
1950	9.562
1955	10,196
1960	14,479
1965	17,206
1970	20,036
1975	60,221
1980	87,012
1985	50,990
1990	53,620
1992	62,919

SOURCE: W. Buhler, *Calculating the Full Costs of Government Regulation* (Washington D.C.: Office of the Librarian, *Federal Register,* 1978). Clyde Wayne Crews Jr., "Ten Thousand Commandments: Regulatory Trends 1981–82 and the Prospect for Reform," *Journal of Regulation and Social Costs* 2 (1992): 114.

to 1980, Reagan had reduced the number by only 17 percent, while expenditures on social regulation actually increased during the period.[17] The most widely accepted estimate of the total costs of regulation in the early 1990s was Thomas Hopkins's figure of $560 billion, dramatically higher than Weidenbaum's estimate even allowing for inflation. Indeed, Hopkins's figure suggests that the costs of regulation were equivalent to 8 percent of gross domestic product.[18]

Everyone, including the authors of these estimates, is aware that they are tentative, not definitive estimates. Moreover, the estimates of the costs of regulation are often produced by committed conservatives (such as Weidenbaum) who are seeking to show that government growth is excessive. No such implication is intended here. The costs of regulation may be well worth paying. The benefits of regulation in terms of lives saved, pollution prevented, or faulty products avoided may equal or exceed the costs. Nonetheless, the estimates do remind us of two useful points. First, the impact of federal government policies on the distribution of resources is far greater—about a third greater—than we would suppose simply by looking at the proportion of GDP controlled by government. Second, the impact of federal government through regulation has increased considerably in the past thirty years. While there appear to be no plausible estimates of the total cost of regulation by the states, they may be considerable. Nearly all states regulate public utilities (natural gas, electricity, telephones), for example, and some states, notably California, have adopted environmental regulations that are more stringent, and therefore more costly, than federal regulations.

National—let alone comparative—estimates of the cost of regulation are open to challenge. Most authorities would agree, however, that American regulation is more extensive and costly than regulation in comparably industrialized democracies.

Do Regulation and Tax Allowances Refute America's Exceptionalism?

There are reasons to suppose, therefore, that the extent of government in the United States is greater than is suggested by the standard measure, the proportion of GDP that government controls. Are the "hidden" aspects of government, such as regulation and tax expenditures, sufficient to cause us to revise the common belief that government in the United States is much smaller than in other advanced democracies? We cannot simply add the costs of regulation or tax expenditures to actual government spending and compare that sum with government spending alone in other countries. Most advanced industrialized democracies have tax expenditures of one sort or another. Britain, for example, offers home buyers concessions such as tax relief on mort gages and the exemption of profits on the sale of one's home from capital gains tax that are even more generous and costly than the allowances given home buyers in the United States. Similarly, all advanced industrialized countries have some forms of regulation.

Yet it may well be the case that tax expenditures and regulation do somewhat reduce, in terms of the proportion of GNP that governments control, the gap between the United States and other advanced industrialized countries. Steinmo, while fully aware of the difficulties in comparing tax expenditures in different countries, believes that they are unusually large in the United States. "There are no reliable international statistical comparisons of the revenue costs of tax expenditures across countries, but both my own studies and interviews with tax policy experts around the world confirm the view that the U.S. tax code has far more tax expenditures than any other tax system in the advanced industrial world."[19] Similarly, most people would agree that regulation in the United States is unusually expensive, although there would be disagreement about whether this reflects greater commitment to causes such as protecting the environment and consumers or merely inefficient forms of regulation. It is frustrating not to be able to be more definitive on these contrasts; we know enough, however, to conclude that comparisons based on the proportion of GNP controlled by government alone exaggerate America's exceptionalism by omitting important types of policies (tax expenditures and regulation) whose costs are not evident from government budget figures.

Areas of Continuing Exceptionalism

There are good reasons to argue, therefore, that the United States is not characterized by limited government to the same degree as some have suggested. Nonetheless, three differences between the United States and most other democracies persist.

The first difference, of considerable importance, is that the United States has repeatedly refused to create a comprehensive system of government-funded health care. The federal government is of course the largest source of money for health care. The Medicare system (providing health insurance for the elderly) and Medicaid (providing health insurance for the poor, including the elderly who have exhausted their own resources but need nursing home care) constitute a significant proportion of total federal government expenditures, and of total expenditure on health care. The government provides no health insurance for the bulk of the population, however.

The absence of national health insurance has two important consequences. The first is its impact on the size of government. If the two-thirds of expenditures on health care that come from private sources came instead from government, an additional 8 percent or so of GDP would count as "government," closing the gap between the United States and Britain, though not the gap between the United States and Sweden. The second consequence is a continuing negative attitude about the role of government. National health insurance would provide another major program (Social Security being the first) that popularizes "big government" because all would expect to benefit from it. As Bo Rothstein has emphasized, the key to the popularity of the Scandinavian welfare state has been universalism;[20] all citizens expect to benefit from programs, in contrast to the situation in the United States, where the welfare state (in spite of Social Security) is thought to benefit "them": racial minorities, undeserving poor people, and single mothers.

It is crucial, therefore, to ask why national health insurance has not been adopted. Some might argue that the absence of such a program is itself proof of America's exceptionalism; alone among the citizens of advanced industrial democracies, Americans have not demanded national health care. In fact, there is no reason to suppose that the American public is fundamentally opposed to national health insurance on principle. Indeed, opinion polls have frequently shown its popularity. It is plausible to argue that the failure to adopt a national health-care policy reflects the power of interest groups (such as many insurance companies) that would lose from its introduction. Moreover, as Steinmo might have predicted, the shortage of tax revenues played a crucial role in ending the prospects of President Clinton's plan to introduce national health insurance. Unable to increase taxes to pay for national health care, Clinton was driven into a plan for mandating insurance coverage by employers that was so complex that the plan became politically indefensible.

Many powerful interests both within the health-care industry and, as in the case of large corporations, outside it, were initially sympathetic to the Clinton plan.[21] Yet at critical moments the public, which had been at first supportive of national health insurance, seemed to waver. In 1994, for example, the longer the Clinton health care plan was debated, the greater the public's uncertainty became. Fears that existing medical arrangements would be disturbed, particularly if change resulted in a reduction in the alleged ability of patients to choose their doctors under current arrangements, resulted in a marked loss of enthusiasm for reform. Some "special interests" may have triumphed, but they did so against a background of widespread doubt and uncertainty about reform. The increasing popular skepticism may have reflected the skill of interest groups, but the most plausible story is one of "path dependency." The United States has evolved a system of employer-financed health care that provides generous benefits for the majority of the population. Beneficiaries of a system that costs them little or nothing directly are understandably reluctant to forgo its benefits for untested models of health care that are usually based in part on assumptions that existing levels of provision for the insured must be reduced to make room for the currently uninsured.

A second aspect of the American welfare state that is distinctive is the limited character of the benefits it provides, a feature exacerbated by the 1997 Welfare Reform Act. Welfare states differ in the length of time and levels of benefits provided, as well as in the basis of entitlement. In his influential work,[22] Gøsta Esping-Anderson has argued that we should categorize welfare states on the basis of access to benefits ("eligibility rules and restrictions on entitlement"), income replacement (how much of previous wages is restored), and range of entitlement (benefits such as unemployment, disability, sickness, and old age). Esping-Anderson also categorizes eligibility in terms of whether it is through means (income) testing, the performance or contribution of workers, or universal rights of citizenship. He then categorizes welfare states according to their scores on a scale constructed on the basis of how restrictive is eligibility, how quickly and for how long benefits are paid, the proportion of normal earnings replaced, and how large a proportion of the population is covered. This yields a "decommodification index" (see table 4.4, p. 76), in which states at the bottom of the list (those having the largest index numbers) are the least restrictive in eligibility, fastest in providing benefits, and longest in continu-

TABLE 4.4

ESPING-ANDERSON'S DECOMMODIFICATION

OF LABOR

Australia	13.0
United States	**13.8**
New Zealand	17.1
Canada	22.0
Ireland	23.3
Britain	23.4
Italy	24.1
Japan	27.1
France	27.5
Germany	27.7
Finland	29.2
Switzerland	29.8
Austria	31.1
Belgium	32.4
Netherlands	32.4
Denmark	38.1
Norway	38.3
Sweden	39.1
Mean	27.2
Standard deviation	7.7

SOURCE: Gøsta Esping-Anderson, *The Three Worlds of Welfare Capitalism* (Cambridge: Polity Press, 1990), 52.

ing them; they provide a high proportion of previous income and cover a large proportion of the population.

Esping-Anderson has argued that the three groupings in the table can be labeled liberal, conservative, and social democratic. Esping-Anderson's categorization is a little suspect and seems driven in part by a desire to label the six lowest ranking countries "Anglo-Saxon" nations, a term reminiscent of General de Gaulle's view of the world. Why Britain is deemed to have more in common with Australia, whose score on his table is only 56 percent of Britain's, than with Italy, with a score almost identical to Britain's, is puzzling.

Yet the United States does indeed seem a very different welfare state from the conservative or social democratic examples. Unemployment compensation in the United States provides a much lower percentage of a person's previous wages and lasts for a much shorter time. Thereafter an American may have to resort to welfare. Welfare benefits offer in turn a lower percentage of average income in the United States than in Europe, and they are increasingly coupled with requirements such as "learnfare," "workfare," or "bridefare," demanding that recipients retrain, work, or either marry or have no additional children in order to maintain their benefits. These requirements are justified as means to secure the early return of recipients to the workforce. They also illustrate, however, how far the United States is from the belief in welfare as an entitlement or right, which is a powerful concept in Europe.

The American welfare state is well summarized by Theodore Marmor, Jerry Mashaw, and Philip Harvey:

> In the jumble of seemingly contradictory goals that have shaped the design of the American welfare state, we believe a more or less coherent set of enduring commitments can be discerned. The income transfer programs we actually have created tend to fall into two categories. They either insure broad strata of the nation's population against impoverishment from the loss of a breadwinner's income, or they assist those whom opportunity has passed by. In other words what has emerged from our ongoing squabbles over the proper goals of social welfare policy is a set of programs that can be described with a fair degree of accuracy as constituting not so much a welfare state as an "insurance/opportunity state."[23]

Of these goals, by far the more important in terms of costs is insurance. Expenditures on programs such as Social Security and Medicare, which the entire populace expects to receive at some point, cost about two and a half times as much as programs targeted on the poor. Perhaps the time has come to focus in our political debates not so much on the desirability of "big government," as on who benefits from it.

The Historical Trajectory

Important contrasts remain, therefore, between the size and scope of government in the United States and in other advanced industrialized democracies. Yet these contrasts should not obscure the contrasts between the size and scope of government in the United States today and in the past. As recently as the 1920s, governments in the United States spent less than 10 percent of GDP. Table 4.5 provides a picture of the transformation of the proportion of national income controlled by government.

The range and scale of government's responsibilities far exceed what was thought appropriate in the past. The contrast between the current American state and the American state of the nineteenth century is far more vivid than the contrast between the contemporary United States and, for example, Britain or Canada. Federal expenditures today are almost double the proportion of gross domestic product that they were prior to the New Deal. Today a citizen can think of one or more of a battery of federal programs such as student loans, federal mortgage loan guarantees, Social Security, and Medicare that affect his or her life or the lives of close relatives. None of those programs existed before the New Deal, and most not until after World War II. As we have seen, the growth in government spending programs has been matched by growth in less visible but equally important government programs such as regulation and tax expenditures.

The adoption of new programs and responsibilities not only has increased the proportion of national income controlled by government but also has produced significant shifts in the relative importance of different programs. The most interesting of these shifts for our purposes has been the transformation of American government from an organization concerned primarily with defense to one concerned primarily with income transfers (see table 4.6, p. 80).

In 1955, expenditures on defense and foreign policy accounted for about three-fifths of federal expenditures; in 1994, the proportion was about one-seventh. Expenditures on Social Security were 56 percent greater than expenditures on defense and foreign policy in 1995; the category of "payments to individuals" as a whole (12.5 percent of GDP), which includes Social Security, overwhelmed the government's spending on defense and foreign policy (4.1 percent of GDP). Thus compared with the pattern in the 1950s, the federal government controlled a larger proportion of the nation's product and used a higher proportion of its budget for income assistance. The argument that the United States is less exceptional than is generally assumed can be supported by observing not only the increase in the share of government revenue as a whole but by observing the growth of social spending by

TABLE 4.5

CHANGES IN GOVERNMENT'S SHARE

OF GROSS DOMESTIC PRODUCT

(GOVERNMENT EXPENDITURES AS PERCENTAGE OF GDP)

	U.S. government figures		OECD
Year	All levels of government	Federal government	figures
1932		11.4[a]	
1936		13.2[a]	
1940		11.4[a]	
1944		n.a.	
1948	17.7	12.1	
1952	26.3	19.9	
1956	24.2	17.0	
1960	26.1	18.3	
1964	27.5	19.0	
1968	30.3	21.0	
1972	30.3	20.1	31.3
1976	32.4	22.1	33.4
1980	31.5	22.3	33.7
1984	32.1	23.1	35.8
1988	32.0	22.1	36.1
1992	34.1	23.3	35.4
1995	32.4	20.9	33.3

SOURCES: Executive Office of the President, *Budget of the United States Government, Fiscal Year 1997: Historical Tables* (Washington, D.C.: 1996), table 15.3. OECD, *Economic Outlook* no. 49 (Paris: OECD, 1991), table R 15; idem, no. 53 (Paris: OECD, 1993); and idem, no. 59 (Paris: OECD, 1996).

a. Calculated from *Statistical Abstract of the United States 1994*, tables 320 and 360.

American governments and, less visibly, the increased pursuit of social goals such as environmental protection through regulation.

Countries can be compared fruitfully with one another and with themselves in earlier eras. In the case of the United States, there is no doubt which method produces the greater contrast. Particularly if we allow for the importance of regulations and tax expenditures, the United States has more in common with most other advanced in-

TABLE 4.6

GOVERNMENT EXPENDITURES BY MAJOR CATEGORY
(IN PERCENTAGE OF GROSS DOMESTIC PRODUCT)

	Defense and international	Net interest	Federal payments to individuals	
			Soc. Sec.	Other
1948	5.5	1.8	0.2	3.5
1952	14.3	1.4	0.6	2.6
1956	10.8	1.2	1.3	2.4
1960	10.1	1.4	2.3	2.5
1964	9.5	1.3	2.6	2.9
1968	9.4	1.2	3.4	2.5
1972	7.3	1.2	4.2	3.6
1976	5.7	1.3	5.3	5.4
1980	5.5	1.3	5.7	4.8
1984	6.6	2.1	6.4	4.4
1988	6.3	2.3	6.3	4.1
1992	5.3	2.5	7.0	5.3
1995	4.1	2.5	7.3	5.2

SOURCE: Executive Office of the President, *Budget of the United States Government, Fiscal Year 1997: Historical Tables* (Washington, D.C.: 1996), table 15.5, 260.

NOTE: The table does not reproduce a column of "other" federal expenditures, which range from .12 percent to 4.6 percent of gross national product.

dustrialized democracies than with itself in earlier eras. We might suppose that powerful continuities in American values over the centuries would have given the United States a distinct pattern of public policies.[24] Far from confirming the general importance of cultural traditions, however, the U.S. experience calls them into question, for the United States, like other advanced industrialized democracies, has embraced "big government" in practice on a scale incompatible with the "liberal tradition" to which it theoretically adheres.

Why Has American Government Grown So Much?

The question becomes, therefore, not so much why government in the United States looks smaller at first glance than governments in comparably industrialized countries but why the U.S. government has grown so much. After all, in terms of both culture and institutions, the United States would seem to provide an uncongenial setting for growth. There is indeed more suspicion of government voiced in the United States than in most democracies, and the institutional system of checks and balances seems to make stopping new policies easier than starting them.

An adequate explanation of why government has grown so much in the United States would constitute a general theory of American politics that would extend far beyond the scope of this book. Several different perspectives on the growth of government exist. Among the most promising are those that might be labeled the inheritance, the democratic, the institutional, the statist, and the neo-Marxist perspectives.

Richard Rose has emphasized the importance of *inheritance* in government.[25] The full costs of many government programs do not develop until long after the crucial decisions have been made. Social Security provides a good example. It was a comparatively low-cost program for many years after its introduction, until the number of qualified recipients increased. What may appear to be a modest change in the structure of a program can have a profound impact on costs. The apparently minor decision in the early 1970s to increase Social Security payments each year by a percentage equal to the rate of inflation had a major impact on that program's cost. A crucial factor in the near future will be demographic change: as baby boomers reach retirement age and people live longer, the elderly proportion of the population will swell. We should be wary, therefore, of assuming that at any particular moment in history citizens or politicians "chose" a different type of state. While in theory politicians could reverse past choices, for example, by abolishing or restricting Social Security, such actions are difficult. Programs such as Social Security, which are not limited to the poor, have a powerful constituency; not even during the Republican revolution of 1994–96 was Social Security endangered. In a way, this is just. Most retirees have based their financial planning on the assumption that the program will continue. Abolition or reduction of Social Security would therefore cause massive hardship. In consequence, politicians today have little choice but to pay for the decisions of their predecessors. Much of the growth was unplanned and unintended, except that past commitments were not reversed.

The *democratic* perspective is at first glance the most straightforward. Americans demand government policies that will satisfy their needs. In a highly responsive political system, citizens' fears of poverty and massive medical bills in old age are assuaged by politicians creating programs such as Social Security and Medicare to prevent these calamities. This apparently naïve perspective has much to recommend it. Attempts to portray American political institutions as unresponsive to popular moods were always unconvincing, even when institutional rules such as seniority appeared to give significant power to a conservative minority. When there was a popular demand for increased government services, they were provided. Moreover, conservative majorities in Congress have never succeeded in rolling back the state to any significant degree at least in part because the most expensive government policies are often the most popular. Did the American state grow simply because ordinary Americans wanted it to? Such an argument overlooks both the ambiguity of public opinion and the apparent continuities in American political culture. It is easy to show in opinion polls that Americans are both in favor of current or increased levels of spending on almost all items in the budget and that they favor shrinking the size of government. Moreover, dominant interpretations of American political culture have emphasized continuity, particularly in its antipathy to a larger role for government. Popular opinion seems an unlikely source, therefore, for an explanation of change.

Institutional perspectives on government growth suggest that the fragmentation characteristic of American institutions offers opportunities for increasing government as well as blocking proposals. Politicians, in this perspective, are credit claimers, attracting votes by taking popular positions. The larger number of politicians in a fragmented political system than in a unitary system like Britain's means that more people can initiate new policy ideas; whereas all major legislation in Britain is initiated by the administration (government), major legislation in the United States may be initiated by the administration or by numerous congressional committees and subcommittees.[26]

Statist explanations of the growth of the state emphasize the actions of "state managers" rather than politics. State managers are "relatively autonomous" from political pressures and are able to use their autonomy to solve problems confronting the state. The genesis of new programs is to be found not in the minds of voters or even politicians but in the actions of people such as senior officials and policy experts.[27] The credibility of this perspective varies according to the type and level of policy in question. A convincing case can be made that foreign policy generally reflects not popular demand but the concerns of state managers. Presidents are often able to obtain popular support for actions such as fighting the Gulf War. Early in the Cold War, American leaders, far from believing that there was a popular demand for the United States to confront Stalin, feared that the public would not support rearmament and a more determined stand against Soviet expansion. Even in domestic policies, voters may more accurately be perceived as demanding that "something" be done than that a particular policy be followed. Most voters had no views, for example, on what the Social Security System should be like before it was created.

The statist perspective is a useful corrective to a tendency to see all policy as flowing from the people, but it too has major difficulties. "Statist" interpreters sometimes seem to ignore political campaigns advocating the adoption of programs whose creation they ascribe to "state managers." Thus, for statist writers, the extensive agricultural subsidy programs created during the New Deal are not the result of twenty years of protest by groups such as the American Farm Bureau Federation and pressure from farmers for policies to rescue them from poverty but the product of state managers. Yet both the identities of state managers and their objectives remain unclear. Are state managers merely bureaucrats? Or are they also politicians, including the representatives and senators who are generally thought to be very susceptible to voter opinion? A particularly difficult question concerns the goals and purposes of state managers. We assume that politicians pursue a mixture of ideals and reelection strategies, while business executives attempt to make a profit. What in general do state managers attempt to achieve?

The *neo-Marxist* account at least provides some motivation for growth in government. The state is managed in the interests of capital, and changes in the needs of capitalists are reflected in the growth of the state. In particular, the growth of the state reflects the needs of capitalists to transfer their costs (for example, for research and development) to the state and to obtain legitimation for the social and political order through the creation of the welfare state.[28] Popular demands for the growth of the state appear in such an account not as an explanation but as a problem for capitalists in obtaining the legitimation that the system needs to survive.

An End to Growth?

The degree to which the size and character of American government remain "exceptional" is a good example of the perennial problem of describing a glass as half full or half empty. Compared with governments in other countries, especially in Scandinavia, American government remains small. Yet government in the United States is far larger than it used to be, and like government in most democracies, it is devoted mainly to making transfer payments, shifting income from one group in the population, such as those currently working, to another, such as the retired. It is instructive to set the percentage of GDP claimed by all levels of government in the United States today (33.3 percent) against those of European countries in 1960, when Hartz's work contrasting the restricted role of government in the United States with European traditions of more extensive government was still new (see table 4.7). Total government spending in the United States today is a higher proportion of GDP than it was in countries with which Hartz implicitly contrasted the United States. In 1960 governments in both Britain and Sweden, for example, controlled a smaller proportion of GDP than the American government did toward the end of the 1990s.

Moreover, the current contrast between the United States and European nations may be diminished when we take into account the policies that do not have a major visible impact on the government's budget but do deeply affect society. The major examples of such policies are regulation and tax expenditures (tax allowances). Regulations cost those who must comply with them far more than they cost government to administer, and tax expenditures do not appear in the budget at all. Yet the consequences of both kinds of policies can be considerable. There are grounds for believing that regulation and tax expenditures are used unusually often as instruments of public policy in the United States. The gap in the size of government between the United States and European nations may therefore be smaller than their aggregate budgets suggest.

Some may argue that the trend for the United States to catch up with other nations has now ended. In this view, the United States was less influenced by the wave of government expansion that began in the New Deal (which was far more adventurous and expansive of government than anything tried in democratic Europe at that time) than by the "neoliberal" reaction against big government that began with the election of Margaret Thatcher in 1979 in Britain and Ronald Reagan in the United States in 1980. The United States was late into the era of big government, and fast out.

This argument, initially plausible, is hard to reconcile with the failure of the Republican revolution of 1994–96. The basic pattern, predictable by political scientists, was that programs targeted on weak and unpopular groups such as welfare recipients were cut, while very expensive programs such as Social Security survived. The expensive programs are expensive because they have a large and effective political constituency behind them; that is also why they survived. When the dust of the Republican revolution had settled, the United States was left with big government.

TABLE 4.7

GOVERNMENT EXPENDITURES AS A PERCENTAGE
OF GROSS DOMESTIC PRODUCT,
EUROPE AND NORTH AMERICA, 1960 and 1995

	1960	*1995*
Belgium	28.4	54.9
Britain	29.5	43.4
Canada	25.3	46.2
Denmark	21.4	62.4
France	30.9	53.7
West Germany/Germany	28.1	49.5
Italy	26.2	51.9
Netherlands	28.6	50.9
Norway	26.4	47.4
Spain	13.7	44.3
Sweden	26.8	66.2
Switzerland	17.2	36.7
United States	**24.8**	**33.3**

SOURCE: OECD, *Historical Statistics 1960–1993* (OECD: Paris, 1995), table 6.4; and OECD, *Economic Outlook* no. 59 (OECD: Paris, 1996), table A28, p. A32.

5

E Pluribus . . . ?

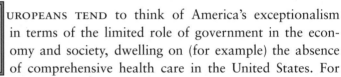UROPEANS TEND to think of America's exceptionalism in terms of the limited role of government in the economy and society, dwelling on (for example) the absence of comprehensive health care in the United States. For Americans, exceptionalism is more likely to imply the story of a land that has brought together peoples from all over the world to make a successful, vibrant society.

The stories that nations like to tell about themselves are revealing to a degree that goes beyond the facts involved. In 1996 the *New York Times* reported that a problem had arisen in implementing a new requirement that city taxicabs play a prerecorded message to passengers at the end of a journey reminding them to take all their belongings with them: there was no agreement on which of the many accents heard around New York should be used in the recording.[1] The story made the front page probably not because this was a crushingly important problem but because it reflected something—diversity—that Americans celebrate as an aspect of their society. In the mid-1990s, the American Jewish Committee ran advertisements in newspapers such as the *New York Times* featuring an image of the Statue of Liberty and a large headline, "It takes all kinds."[2] The advertisement continued: "The tired. The poor. The huddled masses yearning to breathe free. From every corner of the world, from every race, faith, culture and creed we have come or been brought to America. Separately and together, we have dreamed of freedom. And, in America as nowhere else on earth, we have made the dream of freedom real."

The text is classic in two ways. First, it illustrates the practice that so irritates foreigners of unreflectingly, unthinkingly claiming that widely held values are fulfilled in the United States as "nowhere else on earth." Did the writers of the advertisement consider that Australians or Canadians, for example, are just as free as Americans? Second, and more important, the advertisement expresses a widely shared belief among Americans that their nation has been a refuge for those in need or in danger and that it has practiced pluralism, allowing, as the advertisement continued, "that common pursuit [of freedom] by a diverse people."

The immensely popular Statue of Liberty and the museum of immigration on Ellis Island, the landing place for many immigrants to the United States, express the powerful gratitude many Americans feel for the freedoms and opportunities the United States gave their ancestors. It was entirely appropriate that the American Jewish Committee would sponsor the advertisement celebrating American pluralism. If one imagines the experiences of the descendants of two Jews, perhaps brothers, born in eastern Europe in the 1870s, one of whom emigrated to the United States and the other of whom did not, one can appreciate the magic of America. The descendants of the immigrant to the United States would have experienced religious freedom, distressing but by eastern European standards comparatively mild discrimination (being excluded from Princeton but not the City University of New York or, by "gentlemen's agreements," from buying houses in certain neighborhoods), material success (becoming part of one of the most highly paid groups in the United States), and safety. The descendants of the Jew who remained in eastern Europe would have experienced continuing prejudice, the threat of violence (such as pogroms), poverty, limited educational opportunities, and the Holocaust. No one who contemplates such a contrast can dismiss the claims of the United States to be a land of refuge and opportunity.

There have of course been blemishes in this record. Immigration law from the 1920s until the 1960s discriminated in favor of Europeans. The United States did even less than the pitifully little that Britain did to provide refuge to German Jews in the 1930s. Above all, about one in eight Americans is descended from people brought not to a land of freedom and opportunity but to a land of exploitation and slavery. The United States maintained slavery for seventy years after it had been declared unlawful in England, and for thirty years after its abolition in British colonies. Many "ethnic Americans" throughout history, starting with the Irish and continuing to Hispanics today, have been made to feel that they are not "really American." Native Americans were ruthlessly driven westward and harried to near extinction. It is difficult to imagine how to construct a balance sheet that would take account of these departures from American ideals as well as instances when those ideals were honored. But while it is important that failures to honor American ideals be remembered, it is also important to realize that tolerance and appreciation for diversity were sufficient to create in the United States through immigration a population of highly diverse origins. After all, it says something about the tolerance of nineteenth-century Americans that attempts to limit immigration by people whose language, religion, customs, and manners seemed strange came to naught until after World War I, by which time the population of the United States had been transformed.

Cultural Pluralism: A Worldwide Challenge

The United States is by no means alone in facing the difficulties of having a population of highly diverse origins.[3] In a world in which nations once thought to be highly homogeneous, such as Sweden, have sizable minority populations, cultural pluralism and ethnic diversity have become common features of many contemporary societies. In fact, many countries, including those we think of as highly homogeneous, have had more diverse populations than we suppose. The United Kingdom of Great Britain and Northern Ireland is the result of merging distinct ethnic groups and indeed nations, partly by force, partly by agreement (Scotland). The conflict about whether Northern Ireland should belong to the United Kingdom or the Irish Republic has claimed more than three thousand lives since the early 1970s; it has been followed by even bloodier ethnic conflicts in the former Yugoslavia. It is uncertain whether the United Kingdom will survive far into the next century in the face of demands from Wales and Scotland for greater autonomy as well as demands for the separation of Northern Ireland from Britain. Greater autonomy for the Spanish regions (or "nations," as their proponents claim) of Euzkadia (the Basque lands) and Catalonia is even more strongly demanded. Belgium has come close to being partitioned between the Walloons and the Flemish. Our "neighbor to the north," Canada, has been in turmoil since the 1960s

in the face of demands from Quebec for recognition as a "distinct society" or for independence.

The United States is far from alone, therefore, in dealing with an
ethnically diverse population. Indeed, it striking that the United States
faces so few demands for autonomy or independence; unlike many of
the countries just mentioned, the future of the United States as a country is assured. There is no danger that the United States will break up,
whereas it is entirely possible that the United Kingdom, Spain, or Canada will disintegrate. The American method of dealing with ethnic
and racial pluralism has been highly effective. But what is that
method, and how does it contrast with alternative approaches?

The American Way

Although the United States has emphasized the diversity of its peoples'
origins, there are also tremendously powerful pressures toward assimilation.[4] Indeed, assimilation, not diversity, was long the goal of many
Americans. Although Americans came from diverse places, they would
unite to form a single, new race. Herman Melville, the nineteenth-century novelist expressed this powerfully: "You can not spill a drop
American blood without spilling the blood of the whole world. On
this Western hemisphere all tribes and peoples are forming into one
federated whole. . . ."[5] George Washington expressed what was long
the dominant view when he argued that immigrants should not settle
together in groups that would preserve their traditions and language
but should settle as individuals among Americans so that they would
be "assimilated to our customs, measures and laws: in a word, soon
become one *people*."[6]

It is not surprising, therefore, that for many white ethnic groups, a
strong separate identity rarely survives in any profound sense. Richard
Alba has argued that "ethnic experience is shallow for the great majority of white ethnics."[7] Ethnic traditions are rarely preserved; within
a few generations the descendants of German, Italian, and Polish immigrants are all eating much the same food at much the same time of
day; they dress alike, buy similar cars and houses, and have more in
common with people of different ethnicity but similar social class than
with people of the same ethnicity and a different social class. Not all
of this happened "naturally." The domestic science movement, at least
in its infancy, preached the need for immigrants to give up pasta and

the hard, dry, and pungent cheeses they grated on them in favor of soft, orange, and tasteless American cheese. In the end, however, market forces reflected what is presumably a desire for uniformity. As travelers across the United States know, the outskirts of all cities are depressingly similar. The trails of McDonalds and Pizza Huts (intermingled with car dealerships) are ugly, but they provide travelers with the opportunity to eat food that is exactly the same from the Cajun country of Louisiana to the Scandinavian areas of the upper Midwest, from the Irish areas of Boston to the Hispanic areas of Los Angeles. It is frequently not the diversity but the homogeneity of the United States that is most striking.

Similarly, the pressures to conform politically are far greater in the United States than in many other countries. The political system itself is sacred and unquestionable. Every day in school, children are encouraged to pledge allegiance to the political system. Many textbooks used not only in schools but in universities convey the impression that the United States is the only real democracy in the world. Americans are taught that not only the political system but the social system is just. Most Americans are convinced that American society offers more opportunities than European societies—a claim that is highly debatable—and that American society is unusually egalitarian—a claim that it demonstrably false inasmuch as the distribution of income in the United States is unusually unequal.

Although the Constitution (especially the Bill of Rights) claims to guarantee political freedoms, persons outside the mainstream of politics have often paid a high price for their views. Police forces such the FBI have been used not only to monitor but to disrupt the activities of those regarded as too radical. For much of contemporary history, Congress maintained a Committee on Un-American Activities dedicated to rooting out radicalism, at least of the left-wing variety. Those identified as "communists" or "fellow travelers" were denied the opportunity to work in industries such as the movies. In brief, while the United States proclaims its commitment to freedom, the pressures for intellectual conformity have been enormous.

Yet even while there have been numerous glaring examples of the United States failing to honor its officially enshrined values of liberty and freedom for all, those beliefs have served the purpose of promoting national unity and integration. The "civic religion" of the United States provides a unique and strong unifying force. Accepted unquestioningly by nearly everyone, this civic religion, which we may call the "American creed," asserts the distinctiveness and superiority of the government and polity of the United States. In an era in which claims to distinctiveness and superiority on the basis of ethnicity or race (the traditional bases of most nationalisms) are intellectually and morally unsustainable, the American creed provides a more resilient basis for nationalism.

The current status of "diversity" as a goal is therefore a recent phenomenon, and its popularity has quickly prompted concerns about "the disuniting of America."[8] Yet while diversity as a hallowed policy goal—praised by university chancellors across the land—may be recent, the reality of diversity in the United States is not. People of different ethnic origins have lived side by side since the creation of the republic, and as is well known, the history of the United States in the nineteenth century was one of transformation from a nation composed overwhelmingly of the descendants of people from the British Isles to one that was not. In the words of Lawrence Fuchs, the author of the best book on this topic, "No nation in history had been as successful as the United States in managing ethnic diversity."[9] In terms of the relationships between white ethnic groups—though not with African Americans or Native Americans—Americans have indeed been mostly successful and principled practitioners of the politics of accommodation, of avoiding crisis by adapting to each others' needs and concerns. What have been the methods of accommodation? Three methods stand out: limiting the scope for conflict, maximizing opportunities for leverage, and practicing distributive politics.

Limiting the Scope for Conflict

If the American state has propagated the civic religion in which it is sanctified assiduously, it has conspicuously avoided cultural conflicts that might have made the politics of accommodation more difficult. Government in the United States has done little to promote a particular view of what American culture is or should be.

We now take it for granted that there is a separation of church and state in the United States. Although it is true that the Constitution forbids the establishment of any religion, this successful solution to the potential problems of religious diversity was less rapidly achieved than is commonly supposed. When the Constitution was ratified, six of the thirteen colonies had an established religion, and religious intolerance had often been a feature of colonial life. Throughout the nineteenth and well into the twentieth century, practices that would now be thought incompatible with the separation of church and state continued: American children were still saying the Lord's Prayer in public schools in the 1950s. Over the years, federal courts developed the doctrine of a wall of separation between religion and the state, then applied it (along with other federal constitutional restrictions) to state and local as well as federal governments.

Yet, as always in discussing the gap between the theory and practice of American values, we should not cite imperfect application of those values to argue that they were of no importance. The separation of church and state was much greater in the United States than in many European countries (France being the obvious exception). The expansion of religious tolerance in the United States has reflected an important withdrawal by government from potentially one of the most threatening controversies between ethnic groups. Few violent ethnic conflicts in history have been without a religious dimension. By insulating the state from religion, Americans have avoided competition and conflict between groups over which religious creed or church the state should patronize.

Although religious toleration and nonestablishment are particularly important examples of minimizing the scope of conflict, they are not the only ones. The ideal of the public school (if not always its reality) is one that is neutral between cultures and religions even while militantly instilling nationalism through practices such as the daily Pledge of Allegiance, probably unmatched in any other advanced industrialized democracy.[10] European states have been more involved in promoting high culture than the American state, where opera, symphony orchestras, and art museums more typically depend on private philanthropy than government grants. U.S support for the arts increased from the 1960s onward but was quickly engulfed in "culture wars" over whether grants from the National Endowment for the Arts were supporting pornography. The total absence of national educational standards in the United States also illustrates the way in which the role of the federal government in determining cultural standards has been minimized. Recent attempts to introduce national guidelines on what children should learn in history resulted in intense conflict, perhaps illustrating the wisdom of the earlier approach.

Maximizing Opportunities for Leverage

Congress is often associated with interest groups, including the so-called ethnic interest groups. The logic seems clear. Members of ethnic groups, conscious of their ethnic origins, live close to one another and constitute significant voting groups in congressional elections; not surprisingly, legislators are responsive. Legislators representing large numbers of Greek American voters in consequence are active in demanding that the United States punish Turkey for occupying part of Cyprus; those representing large numbers of Irish Americans demand that American administrations be more sympathetic to Sinn Fein (the political arm of the Irish Republican Army); and those representing large numbers of Jewish voters demand that the United States be a loyal ally of Israel.

It would be a mistake, however, to think that ethnic groups are able to work only through Congress. Presidential candidates have sought the support of ethnic groups assiduously since the late nineteenth century. As Theodore Lowi notes, "the Republican platform for candidate William McKinley was directed to these new-immigrant voters with the appeal to "cultural pluralism."[11] Truman's decision to recognize the State of Israel was influenced by his need for votes from American Jews. All presidential campaigns have staffers responsible for seeking support from the major ethnic groups. Until the party reforms of the early 1970s, elected local officials such as mayors had considerable influence in their parties nationally. As elected local officials also having close ties to ethnic groups, they provided another means for articulating the interests and concerns of these groups in national politics.

In brief, the American political system provided a multiplicity of means through which different ethnic groups could articulate their concerns. The minimizing of areas of conflict combined with maximizing the opportunities for influence.

Distributive Politics

The American political system has often been criticized for its inability to make hard choices. A more positive way to view this phenomenon is to say that it has long had a tendency to distribute benefits widely. The absence of tightly disciplined political parties removed the most obvious possibility for overcoming the divided authority of American political institutions. The next most obvious strategy for overcoming the problems of separated executive-legislative authority has been the bargaining ploys of logrolling (promising to support one another's interests or causes in return for support on similar or even unrelated issues). As David Mayhew argued many years ago, the Democratic Party in Congress could be understood as an institutionalized form of such logrolling, occasionally making the bargains more obvious, as when wheat and cotton subsidies were voted on together or when agricultural subsidies were coupled with food stamps advocated by urban Democrats.[12] Lowi has again usefully reminded us that what he terms the First Republic, which lasted for about a century and a half after the adoption of the Constitution, was a "patronage state" that distributed incentives, benefits, subsidies, and licenses but rarely engaged in "direct coercion"—regulation or direct intervention in the economy.[13]

The American state has expanded its role and repertoire of policies. It has not, however, abandoned its attachment to distributive policies. Few legislators fail to ask what the implications of a policy are for their constituents. The Pentagon and defense contractors are eager to spell out what employment will be generated by defense contracts (and the hundreds of subcontracts that major projects comprise) for each congressional district. Nor are presidents (for all their image as guardians of the national interest) immune from the temptations of distributive politics. In 1996 President Clinton lost no opportunity to shower largesse on California, a state that had long been regarded as vital to his reelection. President Ford secured renomination in 1976 by promising Republican delegates to improve Long Island sewers.

Distributive politics can be carried out entirely separately from ethnic or racial politics. White Congregationalists in New York could logroll perfectly well with white Congregationalists in Pennsylvania. But given the tendency for members of different ethnic groups to be concentrated in different places, distributive politics has easily assumed a character that is both geographic and ethnic.

Yet the United States has also benefited from a happy balance. While ethnic groups have been sufficiently concentrated to have gained leverage in elections, they have not been so compacted as to be irrelevant to most of the country or tempted into secessionist dreams. While it is easy to think of areas of the country in which ethnic groups are underrepresented (there are very few African Americans in the Da-

kotas), it remains the case that members of nearly all ethnic groups
can be found in nearly all regions. The problems found in Canada or
Belgium of antagonistic groups occupying distinct territorial areas do
not arise. It is unlikely, therefore, that any group can successfully
claim autonomy or the opportunity to secede.

While distributive politics is usually geographically based, it need
not be. Leaving aside the vexed question of whether affirmative action
programs are morally sound, one can conceptualize them as distributive politics. Although affirmative action was first developed inten-
sively by the Republican administration of Richard Nixon,[14] it has
been expanded and defended since by Democrats. Groups generally
associated with the Democratic Party, such as African Americans, Hispanics, and feminists, have been its beneficiaries. The congruence between affirmative action and the long tradition of distributive politics
in the United States perhaps explains its acceptance in the United
States (and its fervent rejection in countries such as Britain).

Alternative Forms of Accommodation

What other possible approaches to ethnic accommodation, in contrast
to the approaches just described, were not tried in the United States?

One possible approach is denial, for as long as possible, that diversity exists. The population of Britain, for example, originated more
than a thousand years ago as a mongrel nation augmented by waves
of invading tribes reaching the island up to the last successful invasion
by the Normans in 1066. More important, the British have benefited
from waves of more recent immigration that have contributed much
to the nation's prosperity. The Huguenot (French Protestant) refugees
of the seventeenth century brought important advances in textile manufacturing and clock making; Jewish immigrants and their descendants created enterprises that are familiar features of British life, such
as the retail clothing chain Marks & Spencer and the two leading supermarket chains, Tesco and Sainsbury's. Descendants of Irish immigrants have contributed notably to British public life, among them the
Labour prime minister in the 1970s, James Callaghan. Yet the British
persist in thinking of themselves as a nation that until very recently
was highly homogeneous, composed of people whose ancestors had
been on the islands since the dawn of time. A leading nationalist politician in the Conservative Party, renowned for his hostility to the Eu-

ropean Union, is Michael Portillo, the son of a Republican (antifascist) refugee from Franco's Spain in the 1930s.

Unfortunately, this insistence on the false belief that the British are a homogeneous people descended from ancient inhabitants of the islands has made it considerably more difficult to assimilate recent immigrants of different races. The nonwhite proportion of the British population has increased from almost zero prior to the World War II to about 5 percent (about 3 million) today. Yet the fact that Britain is a multiracial society has been accepted very slowly. It is still common to hear black Britons referred to as "West Indians" because their grandparents came to Britain from the Caribbean in the 1950s. Simple racial prejudice is reinforced by popular beliefs that people of a different color "aren't really British," even though they may have spent their entire lives in Britain. Images of national identity often have the effect of excluding certain sectors of the population. A common memory of England is the beautiful sounds of a boys' choir singing in a medieval cathedral; this sound, so moving and evocative for an Englishman abroad, necessarily associates nationality with a religion that is alien to millions of Britons who are Moslem or the hundreds of thousands who are Jewish.

The British are not alone in their denial of diversity. The French have raised homogeneity to a point of principle. French national identity is not defined by race or ethnicity but by adherence to French culture. During the colonial era, the French (unlike the British) insisted that colonies such as Algeria were actually part of France. After the colonial era, the French continued to accept citizens of now independent countries as French as long as they in turn accepted French culture. The president of Senegal could be a member of the Academie Française. Yet this strategy of inclusive homogeneity fails to adapt readily to groups who do not wish to be assimilated. In recent years, numerous incidents have been reported of schools sending Moslem girls home because they insisted on wearing the veil. From the perspective of the school authorities, the wearing of religiously prescribed dress in school violated the strict separation of public education and religion, church and state. From the perspective of the Moslem girls, the schools refused to accept their religiously defined identity.

Attempts by the British and French to deny the existence of distinct minorities pale beside the German tradition. German law defines nationality through descent or bloodline; it is extremely difficult to become a German except by birth to German parents. This reflects a situation in which, as someone who had lived in both Britain and Germany remarked, "The British talk about black British athletes; to talk of a black German athlete would be an oxymoron." The contrast with American practice is clear. The inclusion of groups in the United States has often involved techniques that recognize and reinforce the identity of the groups. The practice of ticket balancing by including members of different racial and ethnic groups on slates of candidates both recognizes their existence and reinforces the existence of those groups through the pride their members can take in the success of members of their community.

A second strategy of ethnic accommodation not followed in the United States is to recognize minorities officially and give them a formal status. It was common in the eighteenth century for European governments to encourage the formation of officially recognized bodies to represent Jews; the British Board of Deputies had its origins in such a policy, and it is now expected that the chief rabbi will be made a member of the House of Lords, where he will sit next to members who are bishops in the Church of England and the moderator of the Church of Scotland. The British government provides almost full funding for religious schools (Catholic and Jewish as well as Church of England) to make it possible for parents to send their children to such schools free of charge just as if they had sent their children to a state school. Significantly, however, state funding has only recently been extended to Islamic schools, in part because of the conflict between prevailing expectations (such as nondiscrimination against girls) and the practices that would prevail in those schools.

The strategy of inclusion by formal recognition of difference is followed most fully in "consociational" societies such as the Netherlands and, until the 1970s, Lebanon. These societies were often described as pillared; the separate communities with their own hierarchical structures created elites who could negotiate harmonious living arrangements with each other. Problems and policies that might produce conflict between the groups were negotiated between the elites representing the different groups; over time, the practice of successful negotiation and accommodation produced high levels of mutual trust.

It is perhaps in the area of cultural accommodation that the United States has been most distinctive and will provide the most important example to the rest of the world. As a consequence of large-

scale immigrations that have occurred in nearly all advanced industrialized democracies, countries once homogeneous now face the need to
come to terms with cultural pluralism. The British solution of pretend-
ing that everyone belongs to the dominant culture and politely ignor-
ing minority cultures and the French tradition of trying to assimilate
everyone into a single culture seem unlikely to prevail. The "pillared"
societies such as the Netherlands, depending on negotiated settlements
between organized cultures, have faced the challenge of the tendency
of the "pillars" to crumble with the decline of religion in those societies. If only by default, the American pattern of distributing opportunity and offering a choice between assimilation and continued ethnic
identity seems the most viable in the contemporary world.

The Future of the American Model

Depressing examples of ethnic conflict from around the world dominate the daily news. The slaughters in Rwanda, Northern Ireland, and
Yugoslavia have reminded us that peace between different ethnic
groups is precious. The success of the United States in achieving peace
between ethnic groups is indeed impressive. Yet few would celebrate
too hard. Events in the 1990s such as the Los Angeles riots or the
sharply different reactions of white and black Americans to the ac-
quittal of O.J. Simpson of charges that he brutally murdered his wife
and her acquaintance were obvious reminders of the racial divisions in
American society. Several different issues called into question whether
the American model could survive.

The first was whether Americans were prepared to extend to
members of racial minorities the opportunities already accorded white
ethnic groups for inclusion in the mainstream of American life while
they retained the group identities and characteristics that they valued.
Would African Americans or Asian Americans be granted the same
opportunities that Italian or German Americans had enjoyed? The evidence is contradictory and therefore supports contending interpretations. Positive developments include the achievement of middle- or professional-class lifestyles by more African Americans than ever before.
More troubling, however, is the decline in the relative incomes of a
much larger number of African Americans, which more than offsets
the progress toward equality resulting from the rise of a black middle
class. It is also disturbing that, as Jennifer Hochschild reports, it is

the more successful African Americans who are the most likely to think that they are denied the opportunity to pursue the "American dream."[15]

The second troubling issue is whether techniques used to pursue racial justice are in conflict with the American creed or unintentionally inhibit the achievement of racial equality. Two policy areas in particular have raised acute concerns: affirmative action and the drawing of legislative district boundaries in a manner intended to secure "majority minority" populations.

The argument about the morality of affirmative action has been so extensive and detailed that there is little chance of resolving it here. The case in favor of affirmative action is that it gives a chance to members of identifiable groups that have long been the victims of discrimination a chance to overcome the consequences of past discrimination such as inferior educational opportunities as well as current prejudices and biases. The case against affirmative action is that it constitutes a departure from core American values—even if those values have been disregarded in past discrimination against these groups—that require equal consideration for all qualified individuals whatever their religion, ethnicity, or race. Moreover, affirmative action produces a climate harmful to minorities, in which it is assumed that any member of a "targeted minority" who secures admission to a prestigious occupation or university did so only because he or she had received special treatment under affirmative action rules.

Does affirmative action conflict with the traditional American approach to cultural pluralism? The answer has to be both yes and no. On one hand, affirmative action can be seen as a retreat from the traditional liberal goal of a society that is "color blind" and treats individuals without regard for their race, gender, or religion. On the other hand, there is clearly much in affirmative action that is compatible with what we have described as the distributive politics of the American model. Ethnic groups in American cities did not demand that jobs and contracts be awarded solely on the basis of merit and price; instead, they argued that people like them should be beneficiaries of government. Similarly, the long-standing practice of "balancing tickets" in elections or appointments to executive branch positions after a change of administration was not a call for the best people to be appointed without regard to their background but an argument that midwesterners or southerners or southwesterners should be represented by one of their own on the ticket or in the new administration. President Clinton's devotion to having a cabinet "that looks like America" pushed him to give tremendous importance in his appointments to the race, gender, and ethnicity of possible appointees. Yet while the *categories* of people being balanced have changed, the practice itself is scarcely new. Whereas it was highly unlikely that presidents in the past worried much about how many women, Hispanics, or African Americans were in their administrations, they certainly did worry about how many southerners or easterners were. There has also been a belief that certain ethnic groups ought to be represented on the Supreme Court. While these practices were incompatible with a purely technocratic quest for the best possible person irrespective of background or origin, they were among the strategies of inclusion that we have described as helping to knot the United States together.

Similar considerations apply to debates about "majority minority" districting. Drawing the boundaries of political units has itself always been a highly political process, one so political that indeed for long the courts refused to enter what they described as the "political thicket" of redistricting. Yet American history has always provided examples of groups seeking to obtain leverage within the political system. This is not to say that the drawing of oddly shaped congressional districts on the basis of the race of their inhabitants is always to be welcomed. It is helpful to remember, however, that struggles to maintain or diffuse the voting strength of particular groups by concentrating or dividing them across wards or districts are almost as old as the United States.

The final danger to the American model to which we are often alerted is the risk that we may lose those elements such as the American creed that have tied citizens of the United States together; we shall be a collection of disparate, fragmented groups. Advocates of "English only" laws, for example, fear that the use of Spanish in the Southwest and Florida is so common that the unity of the United States is endangered. The frequency with which we use racial or ethnic categories in contemporary debates, and the enshrining of those differences in laws or regulations by affirmative action policies, will prevent the gradual assimilation of groups like that experienced by white ethnics in the nineteenth century. Affirmative action, in contrast, rewards people for continuing to think of themselves as different from the rest of the population, rather than assimilating.

While these arguments are not without merit, they are surely somewhat selective in their treatment of American history. German was spoken in Milwaukee at least as commonly before 1917 as Spanish is spoken in Miami today. Television and the need to succeed in national labor markets surely impel ambitious students to acquire a command of English today even more than when labor markets and communities were more local. In a world in which teenagers in Mexico can repeat the lines (in English) from popular American television shows or Hollywood movies, it is surely unlikely that teenagers of Mexican origin in the United States itself will be cut off from English. Finally, no matter how great the differences between groups of Americans seem today, those between nineteenth-century Americans—northerners and southerners, Irish immigrants and WASPs, German Americans, and Russian immigrants—were at least as great. Outside the United States, many fear that local cultures will be homogenized into the American culture, or, to use Benjamin Barber's term, that a McWorld will destroy other cultures.[16] It is odd that in the United States many doubt that the incredibly powerful cultural forces of Hollywood and television so feared abroad will prevail in the United States itself.

Conclusion

It would appear that news of the death of the American model has been greatly exaggerated. If so, the implications for the world as well as for the United States are important. Most advanced industrialized democracies have become much more ethnically, culturally, and racially diverse since World War II. Some 5 percent of the British population is nonwhite; France, Germany, and even Sweden all have significant minority populations. There is no evidence that as yet any of these countries has been more successful than the United States in managing relations between different races or ethnic groups. Seymour Martin Lipset often reminds us in his writings that the best and worst features of American life are connected;[17] the same values that encourage individual success, for example, may also help explain why the United States has a high crime rate. Perhaps a similar observation might serve as a conclusion to this chapter. Americans have clung to traditional beliefs in small government and an individualist ethic even while their government has grown much larger. Yet adherence to traditional beliefs in the United States as a place of refuge and, in general, tolerance, has allowed Americans more success in building a multicultural society than has been achieved elsewhere.

6

Institutions

NOTHING IS more distinctive about the United States than its institutions. Parliamentary democracies are a dime a dozen, the British form having been copied sufficiently often that it has given a name to the type of democracy it has inspired, the Westminster model. In contrast, no stable First World democracy is based on the institutions of the United States. The French Fifth Republic is the only other advanced industrialized democracy with a strong presidency. Yet while the French president has in practice usually been more powerful within his political system than the American president is in his, in theory the system retains a strong parliamentary component so that the government of the day needs a majority in the Chamber of Deputies. It is true that aspects of the American system are admired and sometimes emulated. The Canadians' decision to have a judicially enforceable Charter of Rights guaranteeing basic freedoms was inspired in large part by the American example. The reforms of the British House of Commons that created more powerful Select Committees were inspired in part by admiration for the thoroughness with which congressional committees can investigate problems and policies. In general, however, American institutions stand alone among the world's stable democracies.

It is not the purpose of this chapter to provide a detailed description or analysis of the workings of American political institutions; any number of excellent studies already serve that purpose. Instead, the chapter sets out a number of characteristics that American institutions are said to possess or practices and consequences they generate, and then it asks whether these characteristics and practices are truly distinctive. Different institutional arrangements can often produce similar political practices; the United States is not the only country in which there have been complaints about the tendency of the political system to produce "gridlock." While it is true that no other stable democracy has institutions exactly like those of the United States, it does not necessarily follow that the consequences of its institutional arrangements are exceptional.

Characteristics and Practices

Perhaps nothing is more striking about American democracy than the fragmentation of powers among and within institutions. As all textbooks relate, the writers of the Constitution began this process of fragmentation by creating a system that, as Richard Neustadt emphasized, is characterized not by the *separation* of powers but by their *sharing* between institutions.[1] There is probably no area of public policy where an authoritative decision can be made by a single institution. Although many make the mistake of thinking that the president has the authority to address all our problems successfully, the constitutional reality is that the president has to work in what Charles Jones has aptly termed a "separated system."[2] Even the courts have been an important source of public policy, especially since the Civil War, by pursuing such diverse goals as the justification of the prerogatives of employers against their workers (until 1937) and the protection of the rights of racial minorities (from the 1950s until the 1980s).

It is somewhat less commonly noted that the division of power between institutions provided for in the Constitution has been reinforced by rules and practices that fragment power within institutions in a manner not required by the Constitution.

Congress is the best-known example of the extension of fragmentation beyond the constitutional requirements. Among the procedures and practices that fragment power within Congress are the committee system, the seniority system, the filibuster in the Senate, and a variety of less formalized norms that reinforce these arrangements. The committee system entrusts a considerable degree of power over proposed legislation and the budgets of executive branch agencies to committees that may not always be perfectly representative of Congress as a whole. While this system may expand collectively the power of Congress by allowing its members to specialize in specific topics, there is also a risk that a committee will be dominated by members with an unusually strong constituency interest in its area of jurisdiction; the Agriculture Committees are a familiar example. The seniority system awards the most powerful positions in Congress automatically to the members of the majority party with the longest continuous service on each committee, a practice that limits severely the power of party leaders or the party caucus. Departures from the seniority system by the Democrats in the 1970s and by Speaker Newt Gingrich after the Republican triumph in the 1994 elections reduced but did not end the importance of seniority in the House; it has not been challenged seriously in the Senate.[3] The filibuster, the ever more frequently used tactic of a minority in the Senate to prevent a vote by continuing debate indefinitely unless cloture is voted by 60 percent of the Senate, is a particularly dramatic example of a propensity in American institutions for circumscribing the powers of the majority. Finally, a series of informal, unwritten norms, such as deference to committees, confirm the biases of formal rules. What James March and Johan Olsen have called the "logic of appropriate behavior," the ways in which people are expected to act, reinforces the tendency toward decentralization created by formal structures.[4]

It is important to realize, however, that the fragmentation of power within Congress is but a particularly clear, well-studied example of a more general phenomenon. Although the president is often called the chief executive, his ability to command the executive branch is considerably limited. Not only does regular legislation passed by Congress often contain detailed instructions to executive agencies, but "appropriations riders" attached to annual appropriations bills may contain even more explicit directives on how the money provided is, or is not, to be spent. Proponents of "political control" models of the bureaucracy have emphasized that fear of displeasing Congress—the principal in control of the agents (that is, the agencies)—prompts agencies to follow its preferences. In fact, agencies have multiple principals, which include the House, the Senate, and their committees in addition to the president and the courts. Finally, the process by which executives turn general legislation into general policies or rules is itself circumscribed by the cumbersome requirements of the Administrative Procedures Act. Agencies, far from being free to use discretion, are obliged to hold hearings and create a record that can be used in court challenges to their decisions. The president can pick the administrator of the Environmental Protection Agency and tell him or her to follow certain general policies; the president has the undoubted right to fire the administrator at any moment. But the administrator has been deliberately fenced in by numerous rules and regulations in attempting to turn those policies into specific decisions or regulations.

Consequences of Fragmentation

The often noted and allegedly exceptional fragmentation of American institutions has been both praised and criticized. Fragmentation provides the opportunity for bargaining, much admired by pluralists as a means of ensuring that a wider variety of interests may influence decisions than would occur if decisions were made on a purely majoritarian basis; instead of merely 51 percent prevailing, the need to bargain ensures that a higher proportion of the population has its interests taken into account. The overall levels of satisfaction of the population as a whole will be higher if a larger proportion of the population gains some satisfaction than if only 51 percent of the population is entirely successful.

The criticisms of fragmentation are equally well known: it leads to deadlock, drift, and a failure to resolve the pressing problems of the United States. These difficulties are inherent in the institutional design provided by the Constitution. The House, Senate, and presidency were intended to serve different constituencies, and of course their members are elected in different cycles. Thus these divergent institutions may embody differing concerns if public opinion is changing. On difficult issues, such as energy policy, the House and Senate are likely to represent different interests because they are chosen differently: representation in the Senate is biased in favor of states with small populations, while larger states have more power in the House, where seats are allocated on the basis of population.

In recent years, concern about interinstitutional deadlock has been increased by fears of the consequences of "divided government," the tendency for the various elected institutions to be controlled by different parties.[5] Thus, from 1980 to 1986 the Republicans controlled the presidency and Senate while the Democrats controlled the House; from 1986 to 1992 the Republicans controlled the presidency and the

Democrats controlled both chambers of Congress; and after 1994 the Democrats controlled the presidency and the Republicans controlled both chambers of Congress.

Although there had been earlier periods of divided government (1954–60), the more recent periods seemed to raise more dangerous possibilities for damaging deadlock because the differences between the parties have been more sharply drawn. The contemporary Republican and Democratic parties in Congress disagree more than in previous decades and are more internally united—in other words, there are more "party votes" pitting a majority of Republicans against a majority of Democrats than during the Nixon administration. "Party unity scores" (the percentage of legislators voting with their party) have also increased, in particular for southern Democrats. The ideological differences between the parties became more pronounced as liberal Republicans became scarcer and southern Democrats both shrank in numbers and became more liberal in order to win African American votes. Thus the ballooning budget deficits of the 1980s could be attributed to a standoff between Republican presidents determined to cut taxes and Democratic Congresses determined to maintain major domestic programs. The new conventional wisdom is that divided government produces as much significant legislation as periods of one-party government,[6] which may serve to remind us how rarely in the past party has acted as a strong, unifying force in American politics, even when a single party has controlled both Congress and the presidency. One reason why divided government has attracted so much attention recently is that the parties in Congress are more cohesive and united than in the past. Political parties in the United States have rarely counteracted effectively the fissiparous tendencies of institutions; we have been living through one of those rare moments in recent years.

It is also possible that the new conventional wisdom is wrong. David Mayhew's argument in support of it is heavily dependent on analyses of legislation that passed, and does not take into account legislation that failed to pass.[7] Others have noted that Mayhew's study does not take into account the impact of divided government on the *content* of legislation, diluting proposals into legislation acceptable to both major parties. As John Coleman reminds us, the scholars who were concerned originally about divided government did not argue that *no* legislation could be passed under divided government, but that significant issues and problems might not be addressed adequately.[8]

Institutional arrangements always advantage some interests at the expense of others. In the American context, the normal expectation has been that fragmented power gives local interests an advantage. Seats on congressional committees are generally allocated to those with a strong constituency interest in a question; food and agriculture policy is decided by legislators from rural America, not consumers' America, and military policy is discussed in committees on which sit legislators with an unusually high proportion of constituents who work on military bases or for military contractors. Alliances between these committees and the relevant interest groups also used to result in fragmentation within the executive branch. An agency such as the Bureau of Land Management responded to an interest group (e.g., the American Cattlemen's Association) exerting pressure on it through congressional committees (the Interior Committees) by following policies intended to please the interest group.[9] This alliance between interest group, congressional committee, and executive branch agency was known as an "iron triangle." The end result was the "interest group liberalism" deplored by Theodore Lowi, in which public policy reflects not general values but particular interests.[10]

Most political scientists think that a variety of factors have reduced the prevalence of iron triangles. Three developments are particularly important. The first is pressure from central budgetary agencies (such as the Office of Management and Budget) looking for savings to balance the budget; central budgetary agencies today are less likely than in the past to turn a blind eye to the wasteful policies produced by iron triangles. Second, interest groups have multiplied, and the growth of environmental and consumer protection groups in particular has ended the monopoly on influence that prevailed within iron triangles. To return to our example, nowadays the National Cattlemen's Association must fight environmentalists, and the Bureau of Land Management must try to respond to both. Finally, the considerably increased level of interparty conflict in the United States reflects a greater willingness among legislators to vote on the basis of party ideology, not interest-group politics. The "Class of '94" Republicans, for example, were more concerned with promoting their ideology than with serving interest groups, even those within their own districts. The unchanging factor, however, is that public policy is likely to reflect a variety of interests and pressures represented in a policy network unrepresentative of the political system as a whole.

Representation

Many Americans believe that theirs is either the only real democracy in the world or, if not, then clearly the best.

The primary means by which representation is promoted in democracies is the election. Holding regular competitive elections may indeed be the basic requirement for calling a nation a democracy. Yet elections differ considerably in form and in competitiveness. Politicians in a country operating a system of proportional representation, in which candidates are placed on party lists and in which the share of the vote won by parties varies little, can be secure in their membership of the legislature once they have progressed high enough up the party list. Political scientists outside the United States, such as Anthony King, have stressed that American politicians are more subject to electoral pressures than their counterparts in other countries.[11] Members of the House are elected for unusually short terms (two years); senators serve longer terms (six years) but, to a greater degree than representatives, are likely to face significant primary challenges because there are always established politicians (governors, representatives) who find the prospect of moving into the Senate appealing. It is true that a large proportion—over 90 percent, and sometimes as high as 96 percent—of legislators seeking reelection are likely to succeed; the high success rate of incumbents has sparked demands for term limits. Yet this phenomenon can be interpreted as proof not of the invulnerability of incumbents, but of the successful maneuvering of politicians to adapt to the public's wishes. The behavior of legislators is best understood in terms of the "electoral connection"; legislators maximize their chances for reelection both by providing services to their constituents, such as solving their problems with the bureaucracy, and by modifying their own policy positions.

Representation is, as noted, a core principle of democracy. Yet some believe that representation is taken to extremes in the United States. One criticism is that politicians lack the necessary political insulation to make tough choices. Politicians sometimes need to be able to make decisions that are initially unpopular, even if they are in the long-term public interest. American politicians often lack this insulation and, in King's judgment, are obliged to spend too much time campaigning and too little time governing.[12] A politician voting to increase the gas tax in order to reduce wasteful fuel consumption risks electoral defeat, and in the era of "sound bite" politics, he or she may lack the opportunity to defend or explain such an unpopular choice. In consequence, politics becomes plebiscitary. Second, groups that feel intensely on a subject and that have no organized opposition may have a disproportionate leverage on public policy. Most Americans are in favor of significant gun control; the National Rifle Association (NRA) and its supporters have been able to prevent it. Supporters of foreign countries such as Greece and Israel have been able to influence American foreign policy significantly in favor of those countries;[13] whether it is in the strategic interest of the United States to side against Turkey or to be identified so heavily with Israel is debatable.

In contrast to these views, it can be argued that several political characteristics make achieving representative government in the United States harder than in most parliamentary democracies.

First, the constitutional structure hinders accountability of the government to the governed. The sharing of powers among separated institutions ensures that even moderately well-informed citizens will have tremendous difficulty in determining who deserves blame for a decision they dislike. Consider the problems of a voter determined to punish the politicians in Washington responsible for the ballooning budget deficits of the 1980s. Were the budget deficits the fault of Congress, as President Reagan claimed, or the fault of President Reagan himself? Both the presidency and Congress are involved in deciding the budget. If the deficits were the fault of Congress, was the Republican Senate as culpable as the Democratic House, and how did the actions of one's own senator or representative contribute to the deficit? Few political scientists, let alone typically attentive citizens, would care to determine the answers.

Second, the weakness of political parties precludes voters using one of the most convenient simplifying devices of modern democracy to aid their decisions. A British voter does not need to evaluate the performance of his or her member of Parliament in order to vote intelligently. In a system in which party discipline is very strong, such as Britain's, all that a voter is required to do is determine whether or not his or her MP is Labour, decide what his or her attitude is to the performance and promises of the Blair government, and vote accordingly.

In contrast, the opportunity offered American voters to make separate decisions on who should hold dozens of offices from president to county judge offers no real power to control government wisely, for it assumes a degree of knowledge that voters cannot be reasonably expected to acquire.

Third, American politics is unusually "capital intensive." Most campaigns are fought largely through paid media, with lavish use of consultants and public opinion polls rather than unpaid party volunteers. Public financing plays a limited role and is available only in presidential elections. Parties and politicians are therefore driven primarily by the need to solicit donations; without money, they cannot mount credible campaigns because little or no free television or radio is made available as in other countries. The "golden rule" of understanding parties' policies is therefore, Thomas Ferguson argues,[14] to discover where their money comes from. Both of the parties that dominate American politics receive the vast majority of their funds from rich individuals and corporations. Although political action committees (PACs) have been much criticized in this regard, there are many other less open, less regulated ways in which interest-group money flows to parties, such as the "bundling" of checks from individuals and "soft money" contributions to the parties, a practice that reached scandalous proportions in 1996.

Judicialization

In the United States, Tocqueville remarked in one of his most frequently quoted passages, every major issue becomes a judicial issue. The remark is indefensible as it stands; neither macroeconomic policy nor the major questions of foreign policy have been decided by the courts. Yet Tocqueville's comment is quoted frequently because it contains an important truth. While numerous other countries possess courts empowered to decide constitutional questions even to the point of invalidating duly enacted acts of the legislature, nowhere else are so many matters of passionate public controversy decided by the courts. The famous decisions of the Warren Court reshaping state legislatures and state criminal procedures, the civil rights decisions of the Supreme Court from *Brown* v. *Board of Education* (1954) to the latest decisions on affirmative action, and, perhaps most prominently since *Roe* v. *Wade* (1973), the making of abortion policy by the courts reflect a popular view in the United States that it is appropriate for judges to decide major public controversies. In spite of conservative criticism of judge-made law in these areas, the public generally has more confidence in the courts than in elected institutions. When a former University of Chicago law professor, Robert Bork, was nominated to the Supreme Court in 1987, his judicial philosophy that major controversies should be decided in legislatures, not in courts, provoked a storm of protest from interest groups and most senators; support for Bork's philosophy was much less active.[15]

Although judicial activism is generally defended in terms of the protection of basic democratic freedoms embodied in the Constitution, and in particular in the Bill of Rights, American judges have been found shaping policy in much broader areas than this would suggest. Relying on its power to interpret statutes rather than the Constitution alone, the Supreme Court has decided highly technical policy questions in areas such as occupational safety and health. In one case the Court considered whether benzene could seep through human skin and cause leukemia; in another, it determined what levels of expenditure employers could be obliged to make in order to prevent their employees from suffering injury, illness, or death.[16] Although in these cases the Court's decision could have been changed by fresh legislation because it was interpreting statutes, not the Constitution, in practice it is often politically or practically impossible to change a statute, and the Court's decision, even though based on statutory interpretation only, becomes more or less final.

Tocqueville often stressed the importance of institutions in shaping the mores of Americans. Perhaps the importance of the judiciary in the United States helps to explain why procedural values are so important in American government. The idea of due process is not limited to the courts, but influences behavior in legislatures and bureaucracies as well. While in Britain it has generally been argued that democratically accountable politicians should be allowed to use their discretion, the tendency in the United States has been to oblige decision makers to follow set procedures designed to ensure fairness. Procedural regulations tend to be more conspicuous and important in the United States than in other democracies. Rules play a far more important role in legislating in Congress than in parliamentary systems. Visitors to the United States are often struck by the fondness for procedural maneuvering that can be found in even the most mundane settings. It is by no means uncommon for people even in faculty meetings at American universities to invoke *Roberts's Rules of Order;* this would be seen as an odd thing to do at a British faculty meeting, and there would be no authoritative guide such as *Roberts* to turn to. American bureaucracy can often seem highly inflexible and pedantic compared to bureaucracies in other countries. As James Q. Wilson has explained,[17] this is due not, as right-wing commentators suggest, to the malfeasance, incompetence, or self-interest of bureaucrats, but to the numerous restrictions and requirements placed on them. Procedures must be followed, and consistent treatment maintained. The reason why the well-dressed business executive visiting the United States finds dealing with immigration or customs officials more irksome than at home is that American officials are less free to follow hunches (Americans might well say discriminate) on the basis of their general impression of whether someone is likely to be a terrorist, an illegal immigrant, or a drug smuggler. The foreigner is likely to comment that American officials are so beset by rules that they cannot use their common sense; Americans are likely to respond that common sense is another term for prejudice.

Statelessness

European, particularly continental European, commentators from Marx onward have argued that the United States lacks a proper "state."[18] Once again, the claim advanced in its simplest form is indefensible. The United States possesses all the attributes of a state; it claims a monopoly on the *legitimate* use of force as clearly as any state. Its institutions clearly structure political practices, crucially shaping both a highly distinctive party system and an interest-group system.

When commentators say that the United States has a very weak state or no sense of the state, what they are defensibly claiming is that few if any political institutions enjoy real autonomy from American society, so interests or objectives of the state that are separate from or even in conflict with those of societal interests cannot easily be advanced or defended. One of the most conspicuous examples supporting this claim is the weakness of the bureaucracy. In most democracies, permanent bureaucrats (or civil servants as they are less pejoratively known) play a crucial role in governance. In Britain, for example, senior officials provide elected politicians with policy analysis and advice, taking responsibility for turning the general priorities or commitments of the politicians into policies and warning their political superiors of the probable consequences of the policies they think they favor.

In contrast, the permanent bureaucracy in the United States is cut off by what Paul Light has described as a "thickening" layer of political appointees.[19] The tradition established by Andrew Jackson persists; governance is best handled by citizens from outside government, not by a permanent cadre of professionals. There is, of course, a large bureaucracy in the United States, but the thick layer of political appointees keeps it well away from major decisions. When President Clinton made his unsuccessful attempt to formulate a national health insurance plan, he entrusted its development not to the permanent officials of the Department of Health and Human Services but to a task force composed overwhelmingly of people from outside government and presided over by his wife. In no other advanced industrialized democracy do senior *career* officials play such a small role in policymaking.

As we have seen, it has been common to picture the executive branch as well as Congress as deeply penetrated by societal interests. The idea that the Agriculture Department is controlled by farmers, the Commerce Department by business, the Labor Department by unions is common, if simplistic. Some political scientists concede what they see as the general force of this portrayal of American government, but suggest that there is also a "core executive" of agencies much more insulated from domestic pressures and able to pursue a national or state interest. (G. John Ikenberry, for example, argues that American foreign policy has not been merely dictated by powerful interests such as the oil companies.[20]) Such an inner core might include the Office of Management and Budget (OMB) and the State Department. Yet even in these agencies, the notion of a permanent, continuing state that is separated from society seems to have limited support and to be, if anything, declining. The OMB has long been regarded as the best example in American government of an agency similar to European-style bureaucracy (career officials selected on the basis of merit, educated at the most prestigious universities, continuing in office from one administration to the next). In recent decades, however, the distinctive character of OMB has been weakened; the Nixon administration began the process of reducing the prestige and power of career officials in the agency by introducing an ever thicker layer of politically selected officials from outside government (illustrating the general trend described by Light). This quest for political responsiveness has defeated OMB's prior tradition of "neutral competence."

Another aspect of American government that may be linked to the weakness of the idea of the state in the United States is one that most foreigners find very attractive. American government is much more open than governments in most other democracies. Things that are secrets in other countries are matters of open record in the United States. The Freedom of Information Act, for example, has allowed British researchers to obtain from the American government materials on topics connected with Britain that they have been denied by their own government. This is not to say that there are no secrets in the United States or that no policies being pursued are hidden from the American people; the Reagan administration, for example, provided to right-wing terrorists in Nicaragua (contrary to an act of Congress) funds that it had obtained by selling arms (secretly and contrary to its own embargo) to Iran. The chances of pursuing such a policy for long without detection and damaging criticism are limited, as the example illustrates. In contrast, when the French government had its intelligence services blow up a Greenpeace boat, the *Rainbow Warrior*, while it was in harbor in New Zealand, President Mitterrand received little criticism at home, the French government exerted great pressure on New Zealand to release the murderers from prison, and they were awarded medals on their return to France. While the contrast demonstrated in part the greater militarism in French than in American nationalism, it also reflected a widespread belief in France that it is natural and common for governments to pursue secret policies, particularly in foreign affairs.

But Is This All So Unusual?

American institutions, then, are often thought to be not only distinctive in their form but distinctive in their consequences. The time has come to ask if this is really so.

Fragmentation

The belief that American institutions—separated institutions sharing powers—are more likely to produce discord than parliamentary systems seems well founded, particularly in view of the *intra*institutional as well as interinstitutional fragmentation of power.

It is important to realize, however, that parliamentary systems create a façade of apparent unity that is in fact illusory. No system has been associated more than the British with the idea of cohesive, unified government. Members of the governing parliamentary party are expected to support their government on all important issues. As Donald Searing has noted, the norm of unity exists for the Opposition parties too, though there is no constitutional imperative, as there may be for the governing party, for their members to stick together.[21] Yet scarcely behind this façade of unity are often important divisions. All recent British governments, both Labour and Conservative, have been profoundly split on crucial issues. The divisions within the Major government on policy toward the European Union were fairly well known; the most senior members of the government (the cabinet) were divided between Europhobes (hostile to British membership of the European Union) and Europhiles (supporting British membership). Thatcher's government had been divided on the same issue. Contrary to her image and preferences about how to govern, Thatcher spent the first part of her prime ministership struggling to overcome opposition from among her own ministers (the "wets") to the economic strategy she and her allies (the "dries") favored[22] and the second part fighting colleagues who did not share her antipathy to Europe.

Nor was the Thatcher government unusual in this regard compared with its predecessors or successors. Preceding Labour governments had been deeply divided on almost every major issue of the day. The center-right of the party favored economic and military policies that were regarded as betrayals of Labour's ideals by the left of the party. The prime minister, James Callaghan, kept the leader of the left, Tony Benn, in his government for the same reason that John Major kept his opponents, whom he once described in front of an open microphone as "the bastards," in his cabinet; Major quoted Lyndon Johnson that it was better to have his opponents inside the tent pissing out than outside the tent pissing in. There was also an element of poetic justice in Callaghan's experience of disloyalty from his colleagues. In the late 1960s, Callaghan had campaigned successfully from inside Harold Wilson's government against that government's plans for reforming Britain's then antiquated and unruly unions.

There is less pretense at unity in parliamentary systems in which an electoral system based on proportional representation results almost inevitably in coalition governments. According to Michael Laver and Ken Shepsle, coalitions are the most common form of parliamentary government; most are majority coalition governments (with a majority of seats in the parliament), though there is a substantial number of minority coalition governments.[23] Coalitions necessarily involve bargaining about something; otherwise the coalition would be a single, unified party. In general, coalition governments are thought of as alliances between parties distinguished on the basis of gradations of ideology; a centrist party such as the Freedom Democrats in Germany allies with the center-right Christian Democrats or, less frequently, with the center-left Social Democrats. The price of coalition is a moderation in the policies of the dominant party, following less conservative (or more left-wing) policies than the dominant party would wish. Coalitions may emerge on the basis of bargaining on different types of issues or concerns, not along a single political spectrum. Minority members of a coalition may have a single overriding concern, satisfaction on which will secure their loyalty. The Swedish Social Democrats secured the support of the Farmers' (now Center) Party in return for agricultural subsidies. Israeli prime ministers have maneuvered to hold together governing coalitions by making concessions on issues of acute concern to one member of the coalition, such as whether El Al should be allowed to fly on the Sabbath. In both cases, however, the characteristic of coalition government is the attempt to cement over divisions; often, as in Belgium, Italy, or the French Fourth Republic, the cement soon cracks.

Even when the policy divisions within British governments or between coalition parties are less conspicuous, it remains true that parliamentary governments are likely to be divided. Without regard to ideological differences, British government ministers regularly contend for scarce resources (chiefly money but also parliamentary time) for their own departments. The prestige and standing of ministers both with the officials within their own department and with their political colleagues is determined primarily by their success in these contests.[24] When, on occasion, a minister chooses not to fight for his own department in deference to the wishes of the prime minister or the ideology of the party, the result is not the celebration of that minister; it is instead consternation that the governmental game is not being played properly.

One reason for the frequency with which ministers from spending departments defend their authority is that those departments often feel an obligation to represent interests in the decision-making process. We encountered earlier the belief that American departments and agencies are either captured by interest groups or at least have a symbiotic relationship with them prejudicial to public interests or to the more general goals of an administration. It is too rarely appreciated in the United States that many of the same criticisms are made of spending departments in other countries; the British Ministry of Agriculture, Fisheries and Food was the Whitehall voice of the National Farmers' Union, the Department of Trade the spokesman for manufacturing industry, the Department of Education and Science the loyal servant of the National Teachers' Union. Many of these relationships may have been disrupted by Thatcherism; Thatcher herself certainly believed that such action was necessary because of the overly close relationship between government departments and interest groups.[25] In continental European countries, the relationship between interests and departments has been reinforced by the relationship between parties and interests; in Italy, for example, the farmers' organization backed the Christian Democrats, and the Christian Democrats expected to control the Ministry of Agriculture. The centrifugal tendencies in modern government are by no means limited to the United States; most finance ministries would suggest that spending departments are typically allied with the beneficiaries of their programs against them and other core executive agencies trying to assert the collective values of the government.

Representation

We saw earlier that representation was both a goal and a problem for American institutions.[26] A core value for the system was representative government. While some critics doubted that this was achieved, others feared that excessive representation was a problem for the system. Once again, we may doubt whether American institutions are unique in this regard, however.

Most advanced industrialized nations are governed by what claim to be representative governments. It is indeed true that Americans are provided with an unusually large number of opportunities for participation; the large number of elective offices at state, local, and national levels coupled with the system of selecting parties' nominees through primaries mean that Americans need never go more than a few months without voting in an election.

Participation is not the same as representation, however. A number of features of the American system in comparison with parliamentary regimes make it arguably less representative. The most obvious is that the high value placed on participation in the United States is not matched by participation in practice. Turnout in even presidential elections is notoriously low in the United States compared with turnout in parliamentary elections in other democracies. This may matter less if those who participate are representative of the population in general, but they are not. Indeed, participation declines more sharply as one descends the socioeconomic scale (in statistical jargon, participation is more closely negatively correlated with socioeconomic status) in the United States than in other advanced industrialized democracies.[27]

Finally, as we have seen, the fragmented character of American institutions diffuses accountability. It is much harder to know whom to blame for unpopular policies in the United States than in a parliamentary system. Even a well-informed but angry white male would have great difficulty in deciding whether the president, Congress, or the courts were most to blame for the continuation of affirmative action; parliamentary systems provide a much clearer locus of responsibility.

This is not to say that parliamentary systems necessarily provide better government. Indeed, the concentration of power in parliamentary systems can produce policies that are as damaging as, or more damaging than, those in American institutions.

In parliamentary systems such as Britain's, where one party usually wins an outright victory and can govern without a coalition partner, modest, temporary shifts in the electorate can result in massive but temporary shifts in public policy. The alternation in power of Labour and the Conservatives until 1979 produced a pattern of "adversary politics" characterized by sharp reversals of policy that were deeply damaging to those affected; the steel industry, for example, was nationalized by Labour, privatized by the Conservatives, renationalized by Labour, and reprivatized by the Conservatives in the space of three decades. It is scarcely surprising that it fared so badly in international competition.

The clear locus of responsibility can result in greater tendencies to overload; the propensity of nearly all parliamentary systems to have higher budget deficits as a percentage of gross national product than the United States may reflect difficulties in resisting demands for popular and expensive government services; parliamentary leaders have fewer institutional places to hide than their American counterparts. Competition between major parties for a voting bloc that can provide the margin of victory in a political system in which defeat results in almost total powerlessness can produce frantic bidding for the bloc's votes. Britain witnessed considerable and expensive bidding for farmers' votes between the Labour and Conservative parties in the years between World War II and the 1990s, in spite of the improbability that many farmers would vote Labour. Thatcher's interest in promoting private medical care in place of the popular but expensive National Health Service gave way to fears of the electoral consequences of attacking the NHS. In her last general election campaign Thatcher vowed that the National Health Service is "safe in our hands." Tax allowances that are extremely expensive for the same reason that they are politically unassailable (such as tax relief on mortgage income) survive without significant threat from either major party.

Judicialization

There can be no doubt that the judiciary plays a more extensive and dramatic role in making policy in the United States than in other countries. More interesting than this familiar fact is that whereas the American emphasis on judicially enforceable rights once seemed unusual and outdated, the trend in the rest of the democratic world has been to move in the American direction.[28]

Britain provides an example of this trend. For many years, British judges were limited in the impact they had on public policy. Lacking a written constitution that might be used—as in the United States—to invalidate legislation, judges were limited to applying common law with the help of precedents and interpreting the laws that Parliament had passed; in even these functions, however, the courts were characterized by a high degree of deference to political authority. Much has changed. British membership in the European Union has given judges a higher law that can be used to invalidate acts of Parliament. British adherence to the European Convention on Human Rights has provided British citizens with an opportunity to argue in court that the legal exercise of power by the government conflicted with human rights enshrined in the Convention, just as Americans argue that government action conflicts with the Bill of Rights. Decisions of the European Court of Human Rights do not automatically have the force of law in Britain; legislation is often required to give effect to a decision of the Court, as when it decided that the use of corporal punishment in schools conflicted with the Convention. British governments have nearly always complied with the Court's decisions, however, the exceptions being in the field of counterterrorism. The Blair government decided in 1997 to make the European Convention an integral part of British law, obviating the need to appeal to Strasbourg.

It would be a mistake to think of the activism of British judges as having purely European roots, however. British judges have become more willing to test and overrule the decisions of government ministers through the practice of judicial review. Judicial review in Britain is not the same as judicial review in the United States; it is not a matter of reviewing the constitutionality of statutes but of seeing whether an administrative decision is both lawful and, given the facts of the issue, reasonable. Judges are clearly more prepared to accept applications for judicial review, and to rule against the government in the cases they accept. Not only has the number of applications accepted for judicial review increased, but the anticipation of court challenges has had a major impact on British government. Senior civil servants are now given a booklet, *The Judge over Your Shoulder,* on how to avoid being taken to court; Margaret Thatcher claims in her memoirs that some of the crucial decisions in the development of an unpopular tax that was a major factor in ending her political career were the result of fears of judicial challenges.[29]

No one would suggest that British judges have the power of American judges. The British case is interesting primarily because it displays a trend toward judicialization in a country that traditionally minimized judicial power. Canada has taken a step that Britain is only now emulating. It has created a judicially enforceable Charter of Rights that is superior to ordinary statutes. It is still too early to tell whether or not the Charter will achieve the status of the American Bill of Rights, but that is the intent. Other countries, such as Germany, that have long had a Constitutional Court seem to be experiencing modest steps toward judicial self-confidence in using those powers. A recent decision by the Constitutional Court on the Treaty of Maastricht had an important impact on Germany's foreign policy.

The United States will remain a country in which the judiciary is unusually active and powerful. But whereas this characteristic once seemed odd, even quixotic or outdated, it now appears to be a feature that other countries are cautiously emulating.

Statelessness

Other nations are said to have a stronger idea of the state than the United States. This is obviously true in the sense that the term "the state," which has an unfamiliar, alien air in the United States, would be familiar to political scientists in continental Europe (though not in the offshore islands, Britain and Ireland). The question is whether this difference reflects some underlying reality or is merely a reflection of variations in terminology or intellectual traditions.

The history of the state in western Europe has been one of both growth and decline. The growth has occurred in terms of the range and scale of state activity, particularly since World War II, as the state has come to accept a degree of responsibility for economic management and the alleviation of social problems that extends beyond the level accepted in the past. As we have seen, this is a trend evident in the United States. But the more complete welfare states of Europe, with their clearer sense of accountability for the state of the economy, have produced an even greater expansion of the role of the state than has the United States; as we have seen, although the share of GDP claimed by government in the United States has grown considerably, it remains at levels below the average for the OECD.

It is an error, however, to confuse the idea of a large state with the idea of a strong state. The expansion in the role of the state has come at the price of dependency on powerful societal interests. The Swedish state's assumption of responsibility for maintaining full employment obliged it to accept partnership with labor and employers in neocorporatist arrangements that reduced the state's freedom of action. The state may have played a leading role in promoting economic development in France and Japan. In both cases, however, the state felt the need to recruit interest groups as partners—starting with the Patronat in France and the Keidanren in Japan but working down through networks of trade associations representing specific industries. The state may have been the dominant partner, but it was not an all-powerful partner. The expansion of the British state through the nationalization of industries such as coal mining or the railroads increased the vulnerability, not the strength, of the state. Governments were obliged to pay for massive losses in these declining, unprofitable industries, and they proved vulnerable to strikes. In 1974 the Heath government, challenged by the militant miners' union, called an election on the issue of whether the government or the miners ran the country; the government lost. Perhaps not surprisingly, Thatcher's reductions in the roll of government have been described as a quest for a smaller but stronger state.

These examples indicate two forms of state dependency on societal interests that the United States has not experienced significantly. In the first, the state cannot achieve its objectives without the cooperation of societal actors. Sweden needed to manage an incomes policy; it could do so only with the help of the labor unions, which exacted a price for their cooperation. As the United States has experimented only very briefly with an incomes policy, it has not needed to procure similar cooperation. The second form of state dependency has been the expectation that the state will provide assistance to rectify market failures. In an example that would have been grist for the mill of the "overload" theorists of the 1970s, British coal miners expected the government in the 1980s to pay the industry to produce coal that no one wished to buy; the Thatcher government withstood the strike with difficulty and with scant regard for civil liberties. State assistance to failing industries is not unknown in the United States, as both large-scale agricultural subsidies throughout the modern era and the rescue of Chrysler in the late 1970s demonstrate. Yet neither example demonstrates anything like the vulnerability of the British state to demands for subsidies from socialized industries or, to take an example from what is often regarded as the strongest of states, the inability of the French state to impose international levels of efficiency on Air France. In 1995 the airline staff, joined by workers in other industries, went on strike and the government surrendered.

Most European states display another vulnerability in greater degree than the United States. It is now widely accepted by European states that their capacity to manipulate their economies is much reduced. European nation-states cannot—even when coordinating their actions—maintain the value of their currencies on the foreign exchanges by government action; the amount of foreign currency traded each day on the foreign exchanges is so much greater than the foreign currency reserves of governments that they lack the resources to manipulate the exchange rate. As countries such as Japan and France, in which goverment attempts to identify and promote industries that will be successful in the future, have become more integrated into the world economy, their ability to continue the practice has diminished. The abolition of foreign exchange controls and the creation of a

Single European Market has made it considerably easier to shift investment to the country offering the lowest taxes, least stringent regulations, and levels of worker protection.

In contrast, while the United States has feared what Ross Perot called the "giant sucking sound" of job losses to Mexico because of the North American Free Trade Agreement (NAFTA), it experiences fewer problems in this regard than many European countries. The proportion of American GNP involved in foreign trade is still much lower than for many European nations, so the economy's degree of exposure to these dangers is less. The low levels of worker protection and taxation in the United States compared to Canada have allowed it to poach jobs from north of the border while losing jobs to the south. When the United States does have higher levels of environmental or consumer protection regulations, its international power allows it to exert considerable pressure on its trading partners to adopt American levels of regulation. Finally, the role of the dollar as the basic unit of international finance has offered the United States considerable insulation from pressures from the international economy. Until the 1970s, the Bretton Woods international financial system faced the rest of the world with the choice of either buying American goods or taking more American dollars than they wished to receive in payment for America's deficit; the dollar could not lose value against other currencies. Since the early 1970s, the dollar can fluctuate in value against other currencies, but the United States can still ride out external financial pressures for longer than other countries; other nations have sizable holdings of dollars and may well fear that the United States will respond to any economic crisis by reducing its capacity to protect these countries. Kuwait, for example, has good reasons to avoid a dollar crisis that would reduce the value of its own dollar holdings and produce domestic political pressures for reductions in the military budget. In short, the American state has lost less power so far because of globalization than have smaller states.

One final and unexpected feature of the American state compared with others should be noted. The United States is a country whose continued existence as a state is most assured. Most European nation-states are experiencing significant secessionist movements. The United Kingdom is perhaps an extreme case, fighting both a war with a terrorist organization over whether it retains part of its territory (Northern Ireland) and democratically expressed demands for independence from Scottish and Welsh nationalists. But Britain is not alone in this regard, as numerous other countries face secessionist movements. Examples include Spain (the Basques and Catalans), Italy (the Northern League), France (Corsica), Belgium (Flanders), and of course, returning to North America, Canada (mainly Quebec but also possibly the western provinces). Perhaps the first test for the strength of the state is survival; the United States is unusually likely to pass that test.

Conclusion

Two great dangers in comparative studies are to think either that there is no parallel to be found anywhere else to one's own system or, at the opposite extreme, to exaggerate similarities to the point at which important contrasts are obliterated.

There is little danger that people will fail to notice the distinctiveness of American political institutions. Few countries have copied or are likely to copy the model, so rooted in eighteenth-century thought, of separated institutions sharing powers. The greater likelihood is that people will attribute exclusively to American institutions characteristics and consequences that are features of democratic government more broadly. All democratic systems run the risk of fragmentation and deadlock because the only likely guarantee against these dangers is tyranny. While some institutional arrangements may make deadlock or drift more likely, any democratic system is likely to afford different interests and perspectives in society some means to influence policy.

Americans are in general very proud of their system of government and may have trouble accepting that there are indeed other political systems as democratic as their own. But, particularly in intellectual circles, there is also a tendency to believe that the United States is unusually imperfect, that things are managed much better in Europe, or, more recently, in Japan. Both the nationalist asserting the magnificence of American institutions and the pessimist condemning their failings, however, should take note of the similarities in the character and consequences of institutions. Tocqueville came to America to see the effects of democracy in a world in which democracy was exceptional. In today's world, where democracy is more common, we need to bring an appreciation of its more general consequences to our understanding of American institutions.

7

Conclusion

OW DIFFERENT, then, is American politics? The overall argument of this book is that while American politics is different, it is not unique. The issues, trends, and problems evident in American politics are by and large familiar to citizens of other modern democracies. Indeed, American politics has more in common with the politics of several other advanced industrialized democracies today than with American politics in the past. The share of national income claimed by the state, for example, while below the OECD average, is far closer to that average today than to the share of gross domestic product claimed by the American state in the nineteenth century. Many topics on the American political agenda in the 1990s—the future of the welfare state, taxation, health care, the state of the economy—would be familiar not only to voters in Britain but to voters in most advanced democracies. The sharing of not only ideas but political tactics between British Conservatives and Republicans, (New) Labour under Tony Blair and (New) Democrats under Bill Clinton showed an awareness that there were indeed important similarities in the problems, issues, and politically viable solutions on offer in the two countries.

Of course differences remain, and barriers to convergence are significant. As path dependency perspectives have stressed, choices made yesterday become impediments to convergence today. The enormous number and range of interests with a stake in the current system of health care make it ever less likely that the United States will adopt a system of national health insurance along European lines. Yet the fact remains that although American political *institutions* might baffle the foreigner, the *substance* of American politics would be comprehensible and by and large familiar to an intelligent newspaper-reading citizen of another advanced industrialized democracy within a few weeks after arrival in the United States. Anyone who emigrated from Britain to the United States expecting to live in a land of low taxation would be disappointed. It would be a matter of swings and roundabouts, with savings in some areas and losses elsewhere. Sales tax (or Value Added Tax) would be much lower, income tax about the same, and property taxes dramatically higher in the United States. Even the political cycles of reform and policy stagnation, periods of dramatic change to the prevailing pattern of public policy, and periods of consolidation would—clear differences between political institutions in the United States and in other countries notwithstanding—seem relatively familiar.

If this conclusion is acceptable, it should prompt a host of further questions. The role of the United States in comparative politics and policy analysis has long been that of the Great Exception. Generalizations about comparative political systems have generally been followed by the statement "but not in America." My argument has been that such statements would be expressed more accurately in the form "with minor differences in America." Judged by such criteria as the size of government, the expectations that citizens have of government, and the topics that are debated in government, the United States has more in common with other advanced industrial democracies than with its own past.

The implication of this argument is not that we should revise convergence theory, arguing that all advanced industrial democracies are increasingly similar, but that we should redirect our attention to the sociology of the modern state. Starting from very different points, with very different traditions and institutions, modern industrialized democracies have ended up with similar functions, responsibilities, and problems. The average American expects that the state will be there to help with many of life's expensive challenges, as does the average European. Retirement, unemployment, and even, until very recently, poverty, were seen as appropriate problems for government assistance. Of course major differences, notably national health insurance, remain, but still the similarities among advanced industrialized nations, including the United States, are more striking than the differences.

Few would guess this from political arguments between Europeans and Americans that tend to stress differences, not similarities. A recent article in the sports section of the British Sunday newspaper *The Observer* (4 August 1996) repeated all the stereotypes in explaining American attitudes to the Olympic Games: Americans are atavistic, individualistic, and ruthlessly competitive. By implication, Europeans are more compassionate, collaborative, and caring. It is true that very general statements about the "American creed" can attract support in opinion polls that seem to show that Americans are unwilling to provide for needy citizens. Beyond that very general level, however, as we have seen, the contrasts between generosity and meanness, individualism and communitarianism, fade. The contrasts between the United States and other industrialized democracies are starker when we deal in abstractions than in specifics. Americans are less different than they or others suppose. An implication of this book might well be, therefore, that many Europeans have weaker grounds for feeling morally superior to Americans than they have supposed.

A different implication, however, might be that it is time for Americans to realize that they have left behind the era of small government. While it is true that in the United States there have been significant reductions in the role of government, these reductions have been less radical than in other countries (New Zealand, Great Britain) and have been tightly targeted on politically weak groups such as poor children. Any American politician who thought that there was serious support for ending the really expensive domestic programs of the federal government such as Social Security or Medicare would receive a rude shock in the next election. The striking contrast in American politics is between the rhetoric of small government, on the one hand, and the assumption by large sectors of society on the other that they will be able to benefit from the most expensive programs in the future. Rather like a retiree who insists on dressing like a twenty-year-old, the gap between appearance and scarcely veiled reality is amusing rather than convincing.

Even conservatives have begun to acknowledge the inevitability of "big government" in the United States. The conservative commentator David Frumm has written that "conservatives have lost their zeal for advocating minimal government not because they think it is desirable but because they have wearily concluded that trying to reduce it is hopeless, and that even the task of preventing its further growth will probably exceed their strength. However heady the 1980s may have looked to everyone else, they were for conservatives a testing and disillusioning time."[1] In spite of enormous political strength (holding the White House throughout the period, including eight years of a very popular President Ronald Reagan, and control of the Senate for most of the decade), conservatives achieved no significant reductions in the overall size or role of government. The Republican revolution of 1994 made similarly modest inroads on "big government" except for programs serving the very poorest and politically weakest. In short, the past two decades have been part of the pattern of Americans enjoying the benefits of big government, while politicians who denounce it have flourished.

When Americans describe their society as characterized by self-reliance and small government, they espouse deeply rooted beliefs in the United States that are in no way accurate descriptions of what government in the United States is, or will be in the foreseeable future. Of course many nations believe that they are distinctive in ways that are not true. Most nationalisms and national identities are based on illusions. Does it matter if many Americans believe that their government is confined to a smaller, more limited role than it is? Perhaps not. But several consequences of failing to come to terms with "big government" are worth noting.

One possible consequence is confusion about whether we are debating the total size of government or its components. We tend to confuse arguments about the size of government in general with arguments about the desirability or undesirability of particular programs, such as assistance to poor families. The character of political debate changes when we strengthen calls for cutting back on particular programs by assuming that we are going to change the overall size of government significantly, a goal that, as we have seen, is illusory. By imagining that we are really prepared to dispense with "big government" when we are not, we legitimate attacks on programs serving the least powerful sectors in society.

A further confusion can arise over whether our discontents with government are due to its size or to its inefficiency. People imagine that if government were more efficient, it would be much smaller. This is unlikely. Whether government is actually less efficient than many private-sector organizations can be doubted; very often, apparent inefficiencies, as James Q. Wilson has noted, reflect the loading onto government agencies of numerous competing and conflicting requirements, rather than simple waste or idle employees.[2] The belief that government is large simply because it is inefficient is often used, however, to avoid painful choices. People who resent the overall level of taxation yet like many current government programs convince themselves that if only government were more efficient, it could deliver at least the current level of services at a lower cost; we can keep government programs and cut taxation. This is unlikely. There is no evidence that inefficiency in government is extensive enough to provide for tax cuts, were it reduced; there is also no evidence that the balance of political forces is such that cuts would fall on the least efficient programs.

It may also be that by raging against "big government" in the abstract (while we have no real intention of moving to "small government"), we fail to address significant questions about the role of the state. One of the lessons of the years since the triumph of President Reagan in 1980 is that a whole host of responsibilities that we once thought it indispensable for government to perform are no longer so regarded. The federal government no longer sets airline fares or schedules, as it did in the past. Even such core functions as running prisons are now thought to be transferable to private organizations. Yet here again confusion easily sets in. With rare exceptions (as in the example of ending government responsibility for setting airline fares and schedules), privatization changes the nature of state involvement rather than ending it. When the British sold government-owned industries such as telecommunications, natural gas, and electricity to the private sector, they immediately developed a regulatory apparatus to oversee prices and conditions of service. Privatization did not mean that the price of electricity was set by a "free market," but the role of the state had changed from ownership to regulation.

Nonetheless, there are interesting trends in the forms of state activity. During most of the twentieth century, the responsibilities and size of government agencies have increased considerably. Discussions of "the end of the nation-state" ought to take place against a backdrop of the recognition that the history of the state in the past hundred years has been one of almost continuous expansion into areas —health care, social insurance, economic management, and education—where once its role was very limited. The great question at the end of the twentieth century is whether this trend is now over. From

Sweden to Spain, Canada to Mexico, New Zealand to France, politicians claim to be shrinking the state. Whether this will really happen remains to be seen. So far, the vast, expensive entitlement measures that bring benefits to middle-income as well as working people have proved highly resistant to attack. Republicans in the United States have rushed to defend Social Security just as Conservatives in Britain boasted that they increased expenditures on the National Health Service, even after allowing for inflation. Those who say that they are going to end "big government" may well cut back on the programs targeted on the poor and politically weak; they rarely succeed in cutting the much larger and more expensive programs for those on higher incomes, who enjoy greater political power. The end of big government is probably not nigh.

The crucial point for this book, however, is not that big government is likely to persist, but that attacks on it in the United States are part of an international movement. This is not surprising. Periods of government expansion in the United States such as the Progressive era and the Great Society have generally coincided with periods of government expansion in other countries. The exception is perhaps the New Deal, a period in which the United States was a leader in social reform and government expansion; in some ways, the periods of reform in European states immediately after World War II are the counterpart. The appropriate metaphor to describe trends in the character of the nation-state is that of a convoy. In a convoy, ships sail together, though often spread over a considerable area of ocean. Sometimes ships in the convoy move at slightly different speeds, and perhaps (though this is dangerous) in different directions. By and large, however, the ships move at much the same speed in the same direction. The relationship between the United States and other advanced industrialized countries has been similar. In terms of the development and contraction of government agencies, the United States is toward the rear of the convoy. Yet it is part of the convoy, and the direction in which the American state heads is in the direction of the convoy's other members. It would perhaps take another Max Weber to explain the direction of the convoy as a whole; the beginning of wisdom might be to recognize the commonality, not the exceptionalism, of nations' experience.

Appendix

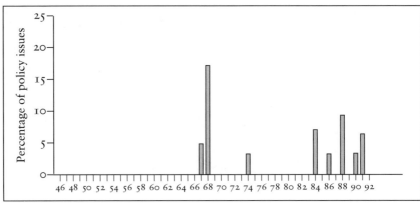

SOURCE: CQ key votes.

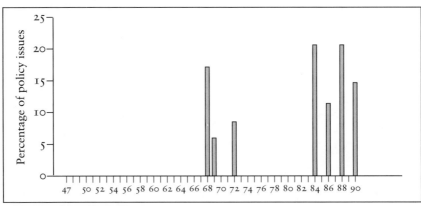

SOURCE: *New York Times.*

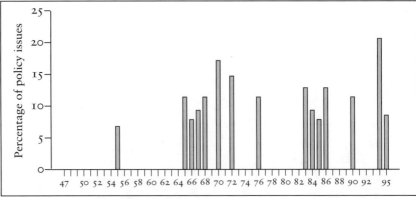

SOURCE: State of the Union addresses.

FIGURE A.I. CRIME / GUNS

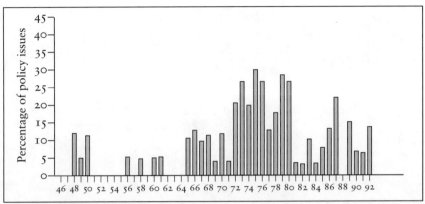

SOURCE: *CQ* key votes.

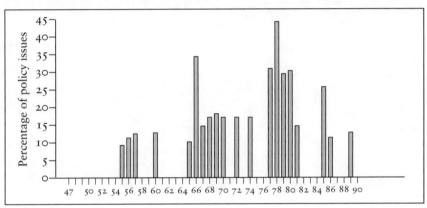

SOURCE: *New York Times.*

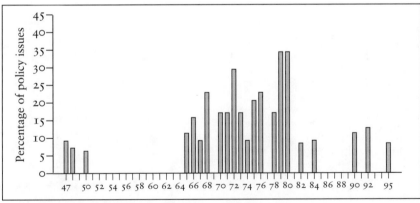

SOURCE: State of the Union addresses.

FIGURE A.2. ENERGY / THE ENVIRONMENT

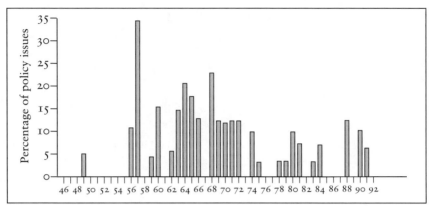

SOURCE: *CQ* key votes.

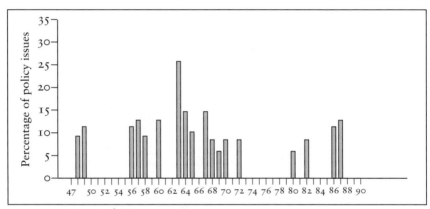

SOURCE: *New York Times.*

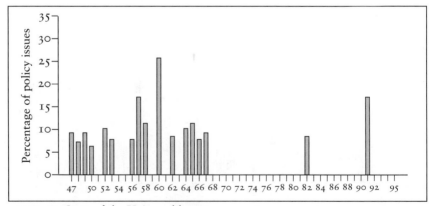

SOURCE: State of the Union addresses.

FIGURE A.3. CIVIL RIGHTS

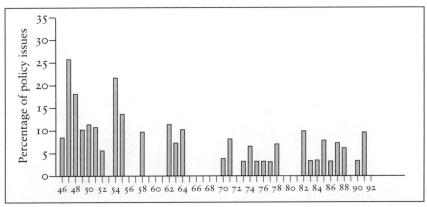

SOURCE: CQ key votes.

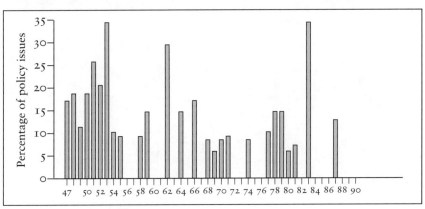

SOURCE: *New York Times.*

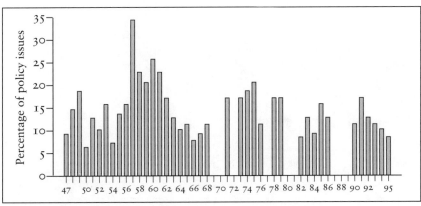

SOURCE: State of the Union addresses.

FIGURE A.4. ECONOMIC AND TRADE POLICY

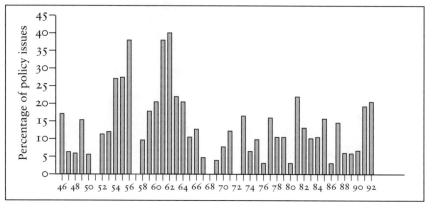

SOURCE: *CQ* key votes.

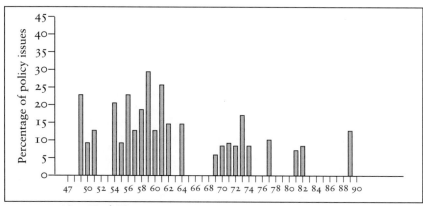

SOURCE: *New York Times.*

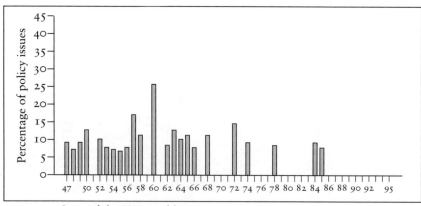

SOURCE: State of the Union addresses.

FIGURE A.5. AID / PUBLIC WORKS

Appendix

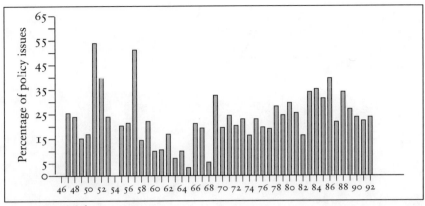

SOURCE: CQ key votes.

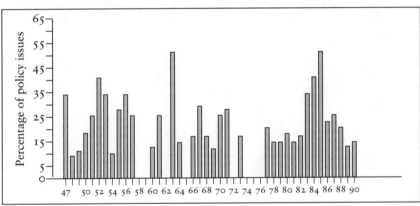

SOURCE: *New York Times*.

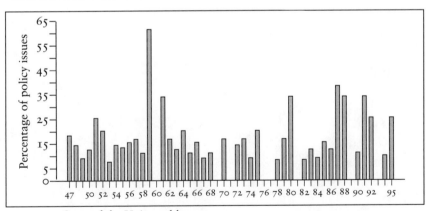

SOURCE: State of the Union addresses.

FIGURE A.6. DEFENSE / FOREIGN POLICY

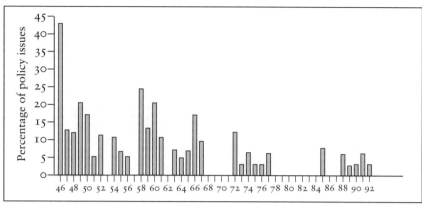

SOURCE: CQ key votes.

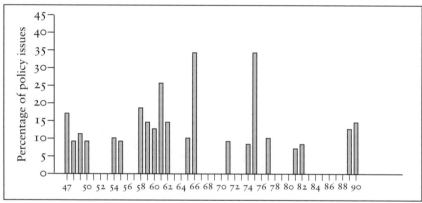

SOURCE: *New York Times.*

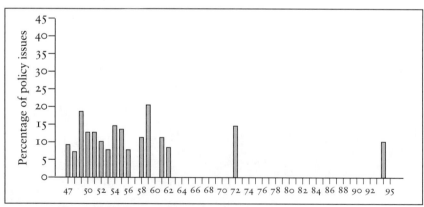

SOURCE: State of the Union addresses.

FIGURE A.7. EMPLOYMENT POLICY

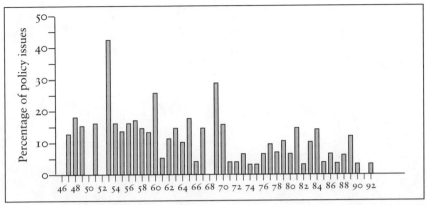

SOURCE: CQ key votes.

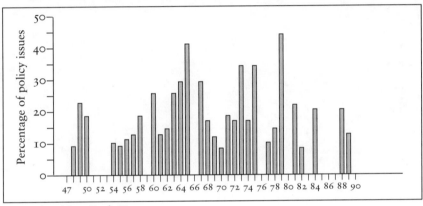

SOURCE: *New York Times.*

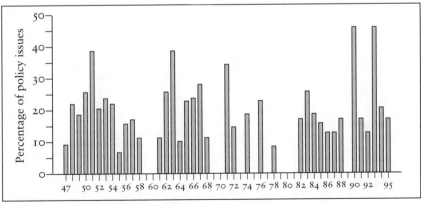

SOURCE: State of the Union addresses.

FIGURE A.8. HEALTH / EDUCATION

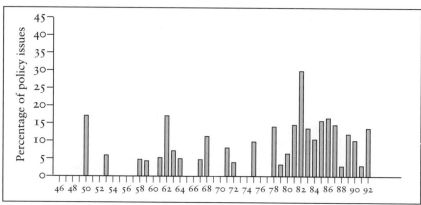

SOURCE: *CQ* key votes.

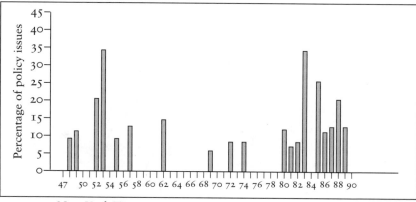

SOURCE: *New York Times.*

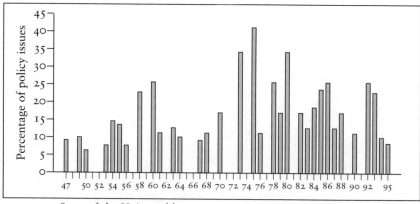

SOURCE: State of the Union addresses.

FIGURE A.9. TAXATION / GOVERNMENT SPENDING

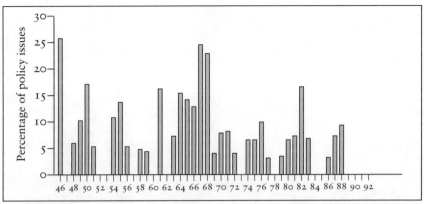

SOURCE: CQ key votes.

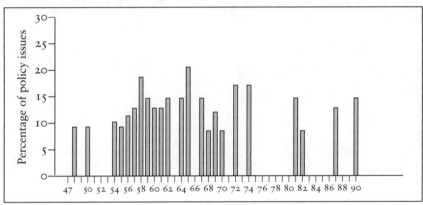

SOURCE: *New York Times.*

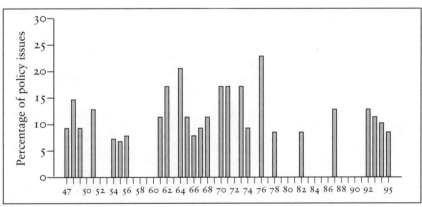

SOURCE: State of the Union addresses.

FIGURE A.10. HOUSING / POVERTY

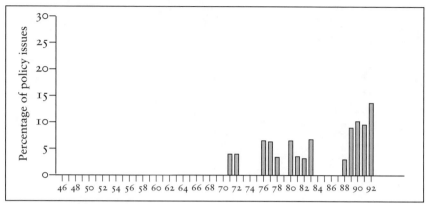

SOURCE: *CQ* key votes.

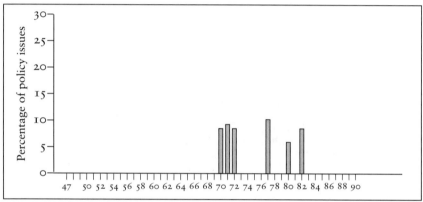

SOURCE: *New York Times.*

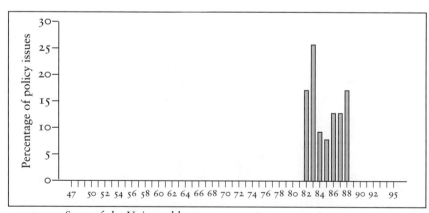

SOURCE: State of the Union addresses.

FIGURE A.11. WOMEN / ABORTION

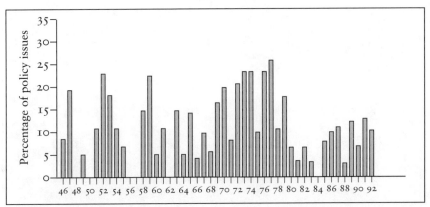

SOURCE: *CQ* key votes.

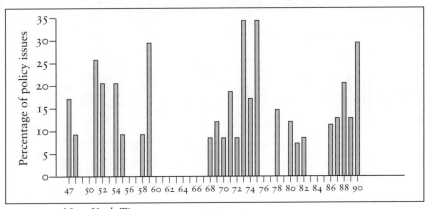

SOURCE: *New York Times.*

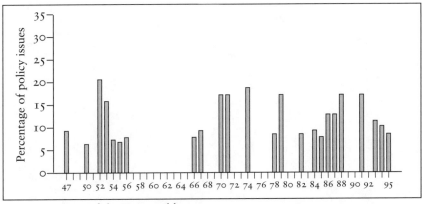

SOURCE: State of the Union addresses.

FIGURE A.12. GOVERNMENT / REFORM / STANDARDS

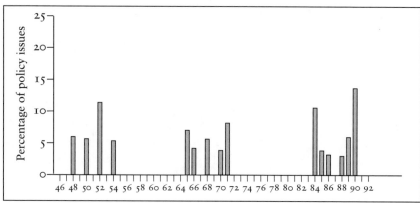

SOURCE: *CQ* key votes.

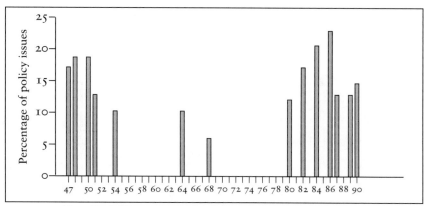

SOURCE: *New York Times.*

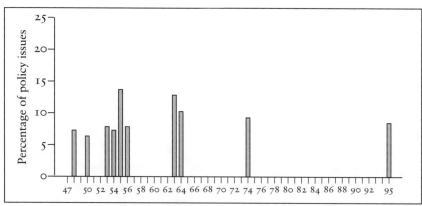

SOURCE: State of the Union addresses.

FIGURE A.13. IMMIGRATION

Notes

Preface

1. *The Spectator,* 24 January 1997.
2. Gøsta Esping-Andersen, *The Three Worlds of Welfare Capitalism* (Cambridge: Polity Press, 1990).
3. Alexis de Tocqueville, *Democracy in America,* vols. 1 and 2 (New York: Knopf, 1948).
4. Werner Sombart, *Why Is There No Socialism in the United States?* trans. Patricia M. Hocking and C.T. Husbands (London: Macmillan, 1976; first published 1905).
5. Louis Hartz, *The Liberal Tradition in America* (New York: Harcourt, Brace, 1955).
6. Samuel Beer, *Modern British Politics* (London: Faber and Faber, 1965).
7. His main work in this area is Seymour Martin Lipset, *American Exceptionalism: A Double-Edged Sword* (New York: Norton, 1996). See also Byron E. Shafer, ed., *Is America Different? A New Look at American Exceptionalism* (Oxford: Clarendon Press, 1991); James Morone, *The Democratic Wish: Popular Participation and the Limits of American Government* (New York: Basic Books, 1990); Richard J. Ellis, *American Political Cultures* (New York: Oxford University Press, 1993); and Robert Wiebe, *Self Rule: A Cultural History of American Democracy* (Chicago: University of Chicago Press, 1995).

Chapter 1. Difference

1. For a useful discussion of some aspects of methodological problems, see Seymour Martin Lipset, *American Exceptionalism: A Double-Edged Sword* (New York: Norton, 1996), 23–28.
2. For one of many descriptions of the American ideal, see Lawrence Fuchs, *American Kaleidoscope: Race, Ethnicity, and the Civic Culture* (Hanover, N.H.: Wesleyan University Press, 1990), esp. chap. 1.
3. For an interpretation of Lincoln's ideas, see J. David Greenstone, *The Lincoln Persuasion: Remaking American Liberalism* (Princeton: Princeton University Press, 1993).

4. L.J. Sharpe, "British and American Conceptions of Democracy," *British Journal of Political Science* 3 (1973): 1–28, 129–68.

5. Lipset, *American Exceptionalism,* 26.

6. Louis Hartz, *The Liberal Tradition in America* (New York: Harcourt, Brace, 1955).

7. Werner Sombart, *Why Is There No Socialism in the United States?* trans. Patricia M. Hocking and C.T. Husbands (London: Macmillan, 1976; first published 1905).

8. Seymour Martin Lipset, "Why No Socialism in the United States?" in *Sources of Contemporary Radicalism,* ed. S. Bialer and S. Sluzar (Boulder, Colo.: Westview Press, 1977).

9. See Henry Aaron, ed., *The Problem That Won't Go Away* (Washington, D.C.: Brookings Institution, 1996).

10. For interesting discussions of agenda setting, see Bryan Jones, *Reconceiving Decision-Making in Democratic Politics: Attention, Choice, and Public Policy* (Chicago: University of Chicago Press, 1994).

11. For a particularly useful discussion of this and other explanations for the failure of socialism in the United States, see Lipset, "Why No Socialism in the United States?"

12. Ronald Inglehart, *Culture Shift in Advanced Industrial Societies* (Princeton: Princeton University Press, 1990).

13. Gøsta Esping-Andersen, *The Three Worlds of Welfare Capitalism* (Cambridge: Polity Press, 1990).

14. Richard E. Neustadt, *Presidential Power: The Politics of Leadership* (New York: Wiley, 1960).

15. For a valuable overview, see G. Bingham Powell, " 'Divided Government' as a Pattern of Governance," *Governance* 4 (1991):231–35.

16. Edward N. Wolff, "How the Pie Is Sliced: America's Growing Concentration of Wealth," in *Ticking Time Bombs: The New Conservative Assault on Democracy,* ed. Robert L. Kuttner (New York: New Press, 1996), 76.

17. The first important study to show this was Seymour Martin Lipset and Reinhardt Bendix, *Social Mobility in Industrial Society* (Berkeley: University of California Press, 1961; revised and expanded edition, New Brunswick, N.J.: Transaction Books, 1991). European societies have almost certainly become more socially mobile since this book was first published.

18. Werner Sombart, *Why Is There No Socialism in the United States?*

19. Fuchs, *American Kaleidoscope,* 23.

20. For a useful source book on the spread of what were once the privileges of wealth to most of the population, see Central Statistical Office, *Social Trends, 1996 Edition* (London: HMSO, 1996).

21. Fuchs, *American Kaleidoscope,* 2–3.

22. Richard Hofstadter, *The American Political Tradition and the Men Who Made It,* 2d ed. (New York: Vintage Books, 1974).

23. Sven Steinmo, "Why Is Government So Small in America?" *Governance* 8 (1995):303–34.

24. Ibid.

25. James Q. Wilson, *Bureaucracy; What Government Agencies Do and Why They Do It* (New York: Basic Books, 1989).

26. Terry Moe, "The Politics of Bureaucratic Structure," in *Can the Government Govern?* ed. John E. Chubb and Paul E. Peterson (Washington, D.C.: Brookings Institution, 1989).

27. Interview, National Public Radio, 27 October 1996.

28. Paul Pierson, *Dismantling the Welfare State? Reagan, Thatcher and the Politics of Retrenchment* (Cambridge: Cambridge University Press, 1994).

29. Richard Rose, *Inheritance Before Choice in Public Policy* (Glasgow: Centre for Public Policy, University of Strathclyde, 1989).

30. Theda Skocpol, *Protecting Mothers and Soldiers* (Cambridge, Mass.: Harvard University Press, 1992).

Chapter 2. Cultural Interpretations of American Politics

1. Louis Hartz, *The Liberal Tradition in America* (New York: Harcourt, Brace, 1955).

2. Gabriel Almond and Sidney Verba, *The Civic Culture: Political Attitudes and Democracy in Five Nations* (Princeton: Princeton University Press, 1963).

3. For an example of such attacks, see Robert Alford and Roger Friedland, *Powers of Theory: Capitalism, the State and Democracy* (Cambridge: Cambridge University Press, 1985).

4. Philip E. Converse, "The Nature of Belief Systems among Mass Publics," in *Ideology and Discontent,* ed. David Apter (New York: Free Press, 1964).

5. Donald R. Kinder and Lynn M. Sanders, *Divided by Color: Racial Politics and Democratic Ideals* (Chicago: University of Chicago Press, 1996), 287.

6. Paul M. Sniderman and Thomas Piazza, *The Scar of Race* (Cambridge, Mass.: Belknap Press, 1993).

7. Kinder and Sanders, *Divided by Color,* 30.

8. Jennifer Hochschild, *Facing Up to the American Dream: Race, Class, and the Soul of the Nation* (Princeton: Princeton University Press, 1995), 55.

9. Kinder and Sanders, *Divided by Color,* 145. Note, however, that only a minority of whites (37 percent) support this general statement.

10. David Fischer, *Albion's Seed* (New York: Oxford University Press, 1989).

11. Ibid., 786, 897.

12. J. David Greenstone, *The Lincoln Persuasion: Remaking American Liberalism* (Princeton: Princeton University Press, 1993).

13. Richard J. Ellis, *American Political Cultures* (New York: Oxford University Press, 1993), 174. Italics added.

14. See also Stephen Holmes, *The Passions and Constraint: The Practice of Liberal Democracy* (Chicago: University of Chicago Press, 1995).

15. Samuel Huntington, *American Politics: The Promise of Dishar-*

mony (Cambridge, Mass.: Belknap Press, 1981).

16. Seymour Martin Lipset, *American Exceptionalism: A Double-Edged Sword* (New York: Norton, 1996).

17. Thomas Ferguson and Joel Rogers, *Right Turn: The Decline of the Democrats and the Future of American Politics* (New York: Hill and Wang, 1986).

18. Fay Lomax Cook and Edith J. Barrett, *Support for the American Welfare State: The Views of Congress and the Public* (New York: Columbia University Press, 1992).

19. Ibid., 62, 65.

20. Ibid., 238-39.

21. Seymour Martin Lipset and William Schneider, *The Confidence Gap: Business, Labor and Government in the Public Mind*, rev. ed. (Baltimore: Johns Hopkins University Press, 1987).

22. Ibid., 210.

23. Ibid., 289-90.

24. Lipset, *American Exceptionalism*.

25. See John L. Sullivan, J.E. Pierson, and Gregory E. Marcus, *Political Tolerance and American Democracy* (Chicago: University of Chicago Press, 1982). A classic exploration of this problem was Samuel Stouffer, *Communism, Conformity and Civil Liberties* (New York: Doubleday, 1955).

26. Richard Hofstadter, *The American Political Tradition* (New York: Vintage Books, 1974).

27. Anthony King, "Ideas, Institutions and the Policies of Governments," *British Journal of Political Science* 3 (1973):291-313.

28. Sven Steinmo, "Why Is Government So Small in the United States?" *Governance* 8 (1995):303-34.

Chapter 3. The Content of American Politics

1. Louis Hartz, *The Liberal Tradition in America* (New York: Harcourt, Brace, 1955).

2. Peter Bachrach and Morton Baratz, *Power and Poverty: Theory and Practice* (New York: Oxford University Press, 1970); Steven Lukes, *Power: A Radical View* (London: Macmillan, 1974).

3. John Kingdon, *Agendas, Alternatives and Public Policies* (Boston: Little, Brown, 1984).

4. Frank Baumgartner and Bryan Jones, *Agendas and Instability in American Politics* (Chicago: University of Chicago Press, 1993).

5. John Coleman, *Party Decline in America* (Princeton: Princeton University Press, 1996).

6. For a discussion of the rise and fall of the New Deal agenda, see *The Rise and Fall of the New Deal Order, 1930-80*, ed. Steve Fraser and Gary Gerstle (Princeton: Princeton University Press, 1989).

7. George Stigler, *Regularities of Regulation* (London: David Hume Institute, 1986).

8. Edward Tufte, *Political Control of the Economy* (Princeton: Prince-

ton University Press, 1978).

9. The banner actually read "Change versus more of the same,/The economy, stupid/Don't forget health care."

10. Theodore Lowi, *The End of Liberalism: The Second Republic of the United States,* 2d cd. (New York: Norton, 1979).

11. Donald R. Kinder and D. Roderick Kiewiet, "Economic Discontent and Political Behavior: The Role of Personal Grievances and Collective Economic Judgments in Congressional Voting," *American Journal of Political Science* 23 (1979):495–527. See also Donald R. Kinder, "Sociotropic Politics: The American Case," *British Journal of Political Science* 11 (1981):129–61.

12. Harold Wilensky, *The Welfare State and Equality: Structural and Ideological Roots of Public Expenditure* (Berkeley: University of California Press, 1975).

13. Gøsta Esping-Anderson, *The Three Worlds of Welfare Capitalism* (Cambridge: Polity Press, 1990).

14. Victoria Hattam, "Economic Visions and Political Strategies: American Labor and the State, 1865–96," *Studies in American Political Development* 4 (1990):82–129.

15. Richard Hofstadter, ed., *The Progressive Movement 1900–1915* (New York: Simon and Schuster, 1965).

16. Ronald Inglehart, *Culture Shift in Advanced Industrial Societies* (Princeton: Princeton University Press, 1990).

17. David Mayhew, *Divided We Govern: Party Control, Law Making and Investigations* (New Haven: Yale University Press, 1991).

18. Richard Franklin Bensel, *Sectionalism and American Political Development, 1880–1980* (Madison: University of Wisconsin Press, 1984).

Chapter 4. The Size of Government

1. United States Bureau of the Census, "Federal Government Employment Data" (http://www.census.gov, 1996).

2. Jonathan Boston, ed., *The State under Contract* (Wellington, New Zealand: Bridget Williams Books, 1995).

3. OECD *Economic Outlook* 53 (June 1993), table R15.

4. For an important earlier discussion of why government is smaller in the United States, see Anthony King, "Ideas, Institutions and Policies of Governments," *British Journal of Political Science* 3 (1973):291–313.

5. John F. Witte, *The Politics and Development of the Federal Income Tax* (Madison: University of Wisconsin Press, 1985).

6. Cathie J. Martin, *Shifting the Burden: The Struggle over Growth and Corporate Taxation* (Chicago: University of Chicago Press, 1991).

7. Jeffrey Birnbaum, *The Lobbyists: How Influence Peddlers Get Their Way in Washington* (New York: Times Books, 1992).

8. Martin, *Shifting the Burden.*

9. Witte, *Federal Income Tax,* table 13.4.

10. Sven Steinmo, "Why Is Government So Small in the United States?" *Governance* 8, no.3 (1995):303–34.

11. The literature is too large to list here, but a good sampling would include Marc Eisner, *Regulation in Perspective* (Baltimore, Md.: Johns Hopkins University Press, 1989); Marver Bernstein, *Regulating Business by Independent Commission* (Princeton: Princeton University Press, 1955); James Q. Wilson, ed., *The Politics of Regulation* (New York: Basic Books, 1980); and George Stigler, *Regularities of Regulation* (London: David Hume Institute, 1986).

12. George J. Stigler, "The Theory of Economic Regulation," *Bell Journal of Economic and Management Science* 2 (1971): 3–21.

13. David Vogel, *Fluctuating Fortunes: The Political Power of Business in America* (New York: Basic Books, 1989); Graham K. Wilson, *The Politics of Safety and Health: Occupational Safety and Health in the United States and Britain* (Oxford: Clarendon Press, 1985); Lennart J. Lundqvist, *The Hare and the Tortoise: Clean Air Policies in the United States and Sweden* (Ann Arbor: University of Michigan Press, 1980).

14. Robert Kuttner, *Everything for Sale? The Virtues and Limits of Markets* (New York: Knopf, 1997).

15. Murray Weidenbaum. "The Trend of Government Regulation of Business," paper prepared for the Hoover Institution Conference on Regulation, Stanford University, July 1979.

16. Murray L. Weidenbaum and Robert DeFina, *The Costs of Federal Regulation of Economic Activity* (Washington, D.C.: American Enterprise Institute, 1978).

17. Murray L. Weidenbaum, *Regulatory Reform: A Report Card for the Reagan Administration,* Formal Publication No. 59 (St. Louis: Center for the Study of American Business, 1983).

18. Thomas D. Hopkins, "The Costs of Federal Regulation," *Journal of Regulation and Social Costs* 2, no. 1 (1992): 5–31. See also Clyde Wayne Crews Jr., "Ten Thousand Commandments: Regulatory Trends 1981–92 and the Prospect for Reform," *Journal of Regulation and Social Costs* 2, no. 4 (1992): 105–49.

19. Steinmo, "Why Is Government So Small?" 306.

20. Bo Rothstein, "The Crisis of the Swedish Social Democrats and the Future of the Universal Welfare State," *Governance* 6 (1993): 492–517.

21. Graham K. Wilson, "Interest Groups in the Health Care Debate," in *The Problem That Won't Go Away: Reforming U.S. Health Care Financing,* ed. Henry Aaron (Washington, D.C.: Brookings Institution, 1996), 110–29.

22. Gøsta Esping-Andersen, *The Three Worlds of Welfare Capitalism* (Cambridge: Polity Press, 1990).

23. Theodore R. Marmor, Jerry L. Mashaw, and Philip L. Harvey, *America's Misunderstood Welfare State: Persistent Myths, Enduring Realities* (New York: Basic Books, 1990), 31.

24. Seymour Martin Lipset, *American Exceptionalism: A Double-Edged Sword* (New York: Norton, 1996).

25. Richard Rose, "The Program Approach to the Growth of Govern-

ment," *British Journal of Political Science* 15 (1985):1–28.

26. For valuable discussions of the impact of institutions, see *Do Institutions Matter? Government Capabilities in the United States and Abroad,* ed. R. Kent Weaver and Bert A. Rockman (Washington, D.C.: Brookings Institution, 1993).

27. There is now a vast literature on "bringing the state back in." The best introduction remains Theda Skocpol, "Bringing the State Back In," in *Bringing the State Back In,* ed. Peter Evans, Dietrich Rueschemeyer, and Theda Skocpol (Cambridge: Cambridge University Press, 1985).

28. James O'Connor, *The Fiscal Crisis of the State* (New York: St. Martin's Press, 1973).

Chapter 5. E Pluribus ... ?

1. *New York Times,* 30 June 1996, A1.

2. For one date on which the advertisement appeared, see the *New York Times,* 18 June 1996, A18.

3. For a useful comparative survey, see M. Crawford Young, ed., *The Rising Tide of Cultural Pluralism: The Nation State at Bay?* (Madison: University of Wisconsin Press, 1993).

4. In this section I have relied on Lawrence Fuchs, *American Kaleidoscope: Race, Ethnicity and the Civic Culture* (Hanover, N.H.: Wesleyan University Press, 1990); Michael Omi and Howard Winant, *Racial Formation in the United States: From the 1960s to the 1980s* (London: Routledge and Kegan Paul, 1986); and Nathan Glazer, *Affirmative Discrimination: Ethnic Inequality and Public Policy,* 2d ed. (Cambridge, Mass.: Harvard University Press, 1987).

5. Herman Melville, *Redburn, His First Voyage: Being the Sailor-Boy Confessions and Reminiscences of the Son-of-a-Gentleman, in the Merchant Service* (Evanston, Ill.: Northwestern University Press, 1969), chap. 33.

6. John C. Fitzpatrick, ed., *Writings of George Washington* (Washington, D.C.: U.S. Government Printing Office, 1938; reprinted 1970 by Greenwood Press), xxxiv, 23.

7. Richard Alba, *Ethnic Identity: The Transformation of White America* (New Haven, Conn: Yale University Press, 1990).

8. Arthur M. Schlesinger Jr., *The Disuniting of America: Reflections on a Multicultural Society* (New York: Norton, 1991).

9. Fuchs, *American Kaleidoscope,* 492.

10. For an interesting comparison of American, British, and French approaches to how to handle diversity in schools, see Meira Levinson, "Liberalism versus Democracy? Schooling Private Citizens in the Public Sphere," *British Journal of Political Science* 27 (1997):333–60.

11. Theodore Lowi, *The End of the Republican Era* (Norman: University of Oklahoma Press, 1995).

12. David R. Mayhew, *Party Loyalty among Congressmen: The Difference between Democrats and Republicans* (Cambridge, Mass.: Harvard University Press, 1966).

13. Lowi, *End of the Republican Era*, 7.

14. John David Skrentny, *The Ironies of Affirmative Action: Politics, Culture and Justice in America* (Chicago: University of Chicago Press, 1996).

15. Jennifer L. Hochschild, *Facing Up to the American Dream: Race, Class and the Soul of the Nation* (Princeton: Princeton University Press, 1995), 251.

16. Benjamin R. Barber, *Jihad vs. McWorld* (New York: Times Books, 1995).

17. Seymour Martin Lipset, *American Exceptionalism: A Double-Edged Sword* (New York: Norton, 1996).

Chapter 6. Institutions

1. Richard E. Neustadt, *Presidential Power: The Politics of Leadership* (New York: Wiley, 1960).

2. Charles O. Jones, *The Presidency in a Separated System* (Washington, D.C.: Brookings Institution, 1994); Charles O. Jones, *Separate but Equal Branches: Congress and the Presidency* (Chatham, N.J.: Chatham House, 1995).

3. James A. Thurber and Roger H. Davidson, eds., *Remaking Congress: Change and Stability in the 1990s* (Washington, D.C.: CQ Press, 1995).

4. James March and Johan Olsen, *Rediscovering Institutions: The Organizational Basis of Politics* (New York: Free Press, 1989).

5. Morris Fiorina, *Divided Government,* 2d ed. (Boston: Allyn and Bacon, 1996).

6. David Mayhew, *Divided We Govern: Party Control, Lawmaking and Investigations, 1946–90* (New Haven: Yale University Press, 1991).

7. George C. Edwards, Andrew Barrett, and Jeffrey Peake, "The Legislative Impact of Divided Government," *American Journal of Political Science* 41 (1997): 545–63.

8. John Coleman, "Unified Government, Divided Government, and the Production of Significant Public Policy," paper presented to the annual convention of the Midwest Political Science Association, Chicago, April 1997.

9. Theodore Lowi, *The End of Liberalism: The Second Republic of the United States,* 2d ed. (New York: Norton, 1979).

10. Ibid.

11. Anthony King, *Running Scared: How America's Politicians Campaign Too Much and Govern Too Little* (New York: Free Press, 1997).

12. Ibid.

13. For the conditions under which domestic lobbies can influence foreign policy, see Mitchell Bard, *The Water's Edge and Beyond: Defining the Limits to Domestic Influence on U.S. Middle East Policy* (New Brunswick, N.J.: Transaction Publishers, 1991).

14. Thomas Ferguson, *Golden Rule: The Investment Theory of Party Competition and the Logic of Money-Driven Political Systems* (Chicago:

University of Chicago Press, 1995).

15. For Bork's views and his account of his experience, see Robert Bork, *The Tempting of America: The Political Seduction of the Courts* (New York: Simon and Schuster, 1990).

16. Graham K. Wilson, *The Politics of Safety and Health* (Oxford: Clarendon Press, 1985).

17. James Q. Wilson, *Bureaucracy: What Government Agencies Do and Why They Do It* (New York: Basic Books, 1989).

18. See, for example, the contemptuous comment that "the American state remains backward," in Bertrand Badie and Pierre Birnbaum, *The Sociology of the State*, trans. Arthur Goldhammer (Chicago: University of Chicago Press, 1983).

19. Paul Light, *Thickening Government: Federal Hierarchy and the Diffusion of Accountability* (Washington, D.C.: Brookings Institution, 1995).

20. G. John Ikenberry, *Reasons of State: Oil Politics and the Capacities of American Government* (Ithaca, N.Y.: Cornell University Press, 1988).

21. Donald Searing, *Westminster's World: Understanding Political Roles* (Cambridge, Mass.: Harvard University Press, 1994).

22. For a particularly good analysis of Thatcher's maneuvering, see Anthony King, "Margaret Thatcher: The Style of a Prime Minister," in *The British Prime Minister,* 2d ed., ed. Anthony King (Raleigh, N.C.: Duke University Press, 1985).

23. Michael Laver and Ken Shepsle, "Divided Government: America Is Not 'Exceptional,' " *Governance* 4 (1991):250–69.

24. The classic description remains Aaron Wildavsky and Hugh Heclo, *The Private Government of Public Money* (London: Macmillan, 1970).

25. Colin Campbell and Graham K. Wilson, *The End of Whitehall: Death of a Paradigm?* (Oxford: Blackwell, 1995).

26. Robert H. Wiebe, *Self Rule: A Cultural History of American Democracy* (Chicago: University of Chicago Press, 1995).

27. Sidney Verba and Gary Orren, *Equality in America: The View from the Top* (Cambridge, Mass.: Harvard University Press, 1985).

28. Herbert Jacob, Erhard Blankenburg, Herbert M. Kritzer, Doris Marie Provine, and Joseph Sanders, *Courts, Law and Politics in Comparative Perspective* (New Haven: Yale University Press, 1996).

29. Margaret Thatcher, *Downing Street Years* (New York: HarperCollins, 1993), 656–57.

Chapter 7. Conclusion

1. David Frumm, *Dead Right* (New York: Basic Books, 1994).

2. James Q. Wilson, *Bureaucracy: What Government Agencies Do and Why They Do It* (New York: Basic Books, 1989).

References

Aaron, Henry, ed. 1996. *The Problem That Won't Go Away: Reforming U.S. Health Care Financing.* Washington, D.C.: Brookings Institution.

Alba, Richard. 1990. *Ethnic Identity: The Transformation of White America.* New Haven, Conn.: Yale University Press.

Alford, Robert, and Roger Friedland. 1985. *Powers of Theory: Capitalism, the State and Democracy.* Cambridge: Cambridge University Press.

Almond, Gabriel, and Sidney Verba. 1963. *The Civic Culture: Political Attitudes and Democracy in Five Nations.* Princeton: Princeton University Press.

Bachrach, Peter, and Morton Baratz. 1970. *Power and Poverty: Theory and Practice.* New York: Oxford University Press.

Badie, Bertrand, and Pierre Birnbaum. 1983. *The Sociology of the State.* Trans. Arthur Goldhammer. Chicago: University of Chicago Press.

Barber, Benjamin. 1995. *Jihad vs. McWorld.* New York: Times Books.

Bard, Mitchell. 1991. *The Water's Edge and Beyond: Defining the Limits to Domestic Influence on U.S. Middle East Policy.* New Brunswick, N.J.: Transaction.

Baumgartner, Frank, and Bryan Jones. 1993. *Agendas and Instability in American Politics.* Chicago: University of Chicago Press.

Beer, Samuel. 1965. *Modern British Politics.* London: Faber and Faber.

Bensel, Richard Franklin. 1984. *Sectionalism and American Political Development, 1880–1980.* Madison: University of Wisconsin Press.

Bernstein, Marver. 1955. *Regulating Business by Independent Commission.* Princeton: Princeton University Press.

Bialer, Seweryn, and Sophia Sluzar, eds. 1977. *Sources of Contemporary Radicalism.* Boulder, Colo.: Westview Press.

Birnbaum, Jeffrey. 1992. *The Lobbyists: How Influence Peddlers Get Their Way in Washington.* New York: Times Books.

Bork, Robert. 1990. *The Tempting of America: The Political Seduction of the Courts.* New York: Simon and Schuster.

Boston, Jonathan, ed. 1995. *The State under Contract.* Wellington, New Zealand: Bridget Williams Books.

Campbell, Colin, and Graham K. Wilson. 1995. *The End of Whitehall: Death of a Paradigm?* Oxford: Blackwell.

Central Statistical Office. 1996. *Social Trends*. London: HMSO.

Coleman, John. 1996. *Party Decline in America*. Princeton: Princeton University Press.

———. 1997. "Unified Government, Divided Government, and the Production of Significant Public Policy," paper presented to the annual convention of the Midwest Political Science Association, Chicago, April.

Converse, Philip E. 1964. "The Nature of Belief Systems among Mass Publics," in *Ideology and Discontent*, ed. David Apter. New York: Free Press.

Cook, Fay Lomax, and Edith J. Barrett. 1992. *Support for the American Welfare State: The Views of Congress and the Public*. New York: Columbia University Press.

Crews, Clyde Wayne, Jr. 1992. "Ten Thousand Commandments: Regulatory Trends 1981–92 and the Prospect for Reform." *Journal of Regulation and Social Costs* 2, no. 4: 105–49.

Dionne, E.J. 1997. *They Only Look Dead: Why Progressives Will Dominate the Next Political Era*. New York: Touchstone.

Edwards, George C., Andrew Barrett, and Jeffrey Peake. 1997. "The Legislative Impact of Divided Government." *American Journal of Political Science* 41: 545–63.

Eisner, Marc. 1989. *Regulation in Perspective*. Baltimore, Md.: Johns Hopkins University Press.

Ellis, Richard J. 1993. *American Political Cultures*. New York: Oxford University Press.

Esping-Andersen, Gøsta. 1990. *The Three Worlds of Welfare Capitalism*. Cambridge: Polity Press.

Evans, Peter, Dietrich Rueschemeyer, and Theda Skocpol. 1985. *Bringing the State Back In*. Cambridge: Cambridge University Press.

Ferguson, Thomas. 1995. *Golden Rule: The Investment Theory of Party Competition and the Logic of Money-Driven Political Systems*. Chicago: University of Chicago Press.

Ferguson, Thomas, and Joel Rogers. 1986. *Right Turn: The Decline of the Democrats and the Future of American Politics*. New York: Hill and Wang.

Fiorina, Morris. 1996. *Divided Government*. 2d ed. Boston: Allyn and Bacon.

Fischer, David Hackett. 1989. *Albion's Seed: Four British Folkways in America*. New York: Oxford University Press.

Fraser, Steve, and Gary Gerstle, eds. 1989. *The Rise and Fall of the New Deal Order, 1930–1980*. Princeton: Princeton University Press.

Frumm, David. 1994. *Dead Right*. New York: Basic Books.

Fuchs, Lawrence. 1990. *American Kaleidoscope: Race, Ethnicity and the Civic Culture*. Hanover, N.H.: Wesleyan University Press.

Glazer, Nathan. 1987. *Affirmative Discrimination: Ethnic Inequality and Public Policy*. 2d ed. Cambridge, Mass.: Harvard University Press.

Greenstone, J. David. 1993. *The Lincoln Persuasion: Remaking American Liberalism*. Princeton: Princeton University Press.

Hartz, Louis. 1955. *The Liberal Tradition in America*. New York: Harcourt,

References

Brace.

Hattam, Victoria. 1990. "Economic Visions and Political Strategies: American Labor and the State, 1865–96." *Studies in American Political Development* 4:82–129.

Hochschild, Jennifer. 1995. *Facing Up to the American Dream: Race, Class, and the Soul of the Nation*. Princeton: Princeton University Press.

Hofstadter, Richard. 1994. *The American Political Tradition and the Men Who Made It*, 2d ed. New York: Vintage Books.

———. 1965. *The Progressive Movement, 1900–1915*. New York: Simon and Schuster.

Holmes, Stephen. 1995. *The Passions and Constraint: The Practice of Liberal Democracy*. Chicago: University of Chicago Press.

Hopkins, Thomas D. 1992. "The Costs of Federal Regulation." *Journal of Regulation and Social Costs* 2:5–31.

Huntington, Samuel. 1981. *American Politics: The Promise of Disharmony*. Cambridge, Mass.: Belknap Press.

Ikenberry, G. John. 1988. *Reasons of State: Oil Politics and the Capacities of American Government*. Ithaca, N.Y.: Cornell University Press.

Inglehart, Ronald. 1990. *Culture Shift in Advanced Industrial Societies*. Princeton: Princeton University Press.

Jacob, Herbert, Erhard Blankenburg, Herbert M. Kritzer, Doris Marie Provine, and Joseph Sanders. 1996. *Courts, Law and Politics in Comparative Perspective*. New Haven: Yale University Press.

Jones, Bryan. 1994. *Reconceiving Decision-Making in Democratic Politics: Attention, Choice, and Public Policy*. Chicago: University of Chicago Press.

Jones, Charles O. 1994. *The Presidency in a Separated System*. Washington, D.C.: Brookings Institution.

———. 1995. *Separate but Equal Branches: Congress and the Presidency*. Chatham, N.J.: Chatham House.

Kammen, Michael. 1993. "The Problem of American Exceptionalism." *American Quarterly* 45, no. 1:1–43.

Kinder, Donald R. 1981. "Sociotropic Politics: The American Case." *British Journal of Political Science* 11:129–61.

Kinder, Donald, and D. Roderick Kiewiet. 1979. "Economic Discontent and Political Behavior: The Role of Personal Grievances and Collective Economic Judgments in Congressional Voting." *American Journal of Political Science* 23:495–527.

Kinder, Donald R., and Lynn M. Sanders. 1996. *Divided by Color: Racial Politics and Democratic Ideals*. Chicago: University of Chicago Press.

King, Anthony. 1973. "Ideas, Institutions and the Policies of Governments." *British Journal of Political Science* 3:291–313.

———. 1985. "Margaret Thatcher: The Style of a Prime Minister." In *The British Prime Minister*, 2d ed., ed. Anthony King. Raleigh, N.C.: Duke University Press.

———. 1997. *Running Scared: How America's Politicians Campaign Too Much and Govern Too Little*. New York: Free Press.

Kingdon, John. 1984. *Agendas, Alternatives and Public Policies*. Boston: Little, Brown.

Kuttner, Robert. 1997. *Everything for Sale? The Virtues and Limits of Markets*. New York: Knopf.

Ladd, Everett. 1994. *The American Ideology*. Storrs, Conn.: Roper Center for Public Opinion Research.

Laver, Michael, and Ken Shepsle. 1991. "Divided Government: America Is Not 'Exceptional.'" *Governance* 4:240–69.

Levinson, Meira. 1997. "Liberalism versus Democracy? Schooling Private Citizens in the Public Sphere." *British Journal of Political Science* 27:333–60.

Light, Paul. 1995. *Thickening Government: Federal Hierarchy and the Diffusion of Accountability*. Washington, D.C.: Brookings Institution.

Lipset, Seymour Martin. 1996. *American Exceptionalism: A Double-Edged Sword*. New York: Norton.

Lipset, Seymour Martin, and Reinhardt Bendix. 1961 and 1991. *Social Mobility in Industrial Society*. Berkeley: University of California Press; rev. and expanded, New Brunswick, N.J.: Transaction Books.

Lipset, Seymour Martin, and William Schneider. 1987. *The Confidence Gap: Business, Labor and Government in the Public Mind*. Rev. ed. Baltimore, Md.: Johns Hopkins University Press.

Lowi, Theodore. 1979. *The End of Liberalism: The Second Republic of the United States*. 2d ed. New York: Norton.

———. 1995. *The End of the Republican Era*. Norman: University of Oklahoma Press.

Lukes, Steven. 1974. *Power: A Radical View*. London: Macmillan.

Lundqvist, Lennart J. 1980. *The Hare and the Tortoise: Clean Air Policies in the United States and Sweden*. Ann Arbor: University of Michigan Press.

March, James, and Johan Olsen. 1989. *Rediscovering Institutions: The Organizational Basis of Politics*. New York: Free Press.

Marmor, Theodore, Jerry L. Mashaw, and Philip L. Harvey. 1990. *America's Misunderstood Welfare State: Persistent Myths, Enduring Realities*. New York: Basic Books.

Martin, Cathie Jo. 1991. *Shifting the Burden: The Struggle over Growth and Corporate Taxation*. Chicago: University of Chicago Press.

Mayhew, David R. 1966. *Party Loyalty among Congressmen: The Difference between Democrats and Republicans, 1947–1962*. Cambridge, Mass.: Harvard University Press.

———. 1991. *Divided We Govern: Party Control, Law Making and Investigations 1946–90*. New Haven: Yale University Press.

Moe, Terry. 1989. "The Politics of Bureaucratic Structure." In *Can the Government Govern?* ed. John E. Chubb and Paul E. Peterson. Washington, D.C.: Brookings Institution.

Morone, James. 1990. *The Democratic Wish: Popular Participation and the Limits of American Government*. New York: Basic Books.

Neustadt, Richard E. 1960. *Presidential Power: The Politics of Leadership*.

References

New York: Wiley.

O'Connor, James. 1973. *The Fiscal Crisis of the State.* New York: St. Martin's Press.

Omi, Michael, and Howard Winant. 1986. *Racial Formation in the United States: From the 1960s to the 1980s.* London: Routledge and Kegan Paul.

Pierson, Paul. 1994. *Dismantling the Welfare State? Reagan, Thatcher and the Politics of Retrenchment.* Cambridge: Cambridge University Press.

Powell, G. Bingham. 1991. " 'Divided Government' as a Pattern of Government." *Governance* 4:231–35.

Rose, Richard. 1985. "The Program Approach to the Growth of Government." *British Journal of Political Science* 15:1–28.

———. 1989. *Inheritance Before Choice in Public Policy.* Glasgow: Centre for Public Policy, University of Strathclyde.

Rothstein, Bo. 1993. "The Crisis of the Swedish Social Democrats and the Future of the Universal Welfare State." *Governance* 6:492–517.

Schlesinger, Arthur M., Jr. 1991. *The Disuniting of America: Reflections on a Multicultural Society.* New York: Norton.

Searing, Donald. 1994. *Westminster's World: Understanding Political Roles.* Cambridge, Mass.: Harvard University Press.

Shafer, Byron, ed. 1991. *Is America Different? A New Look at American Exceptionalism.* Oxford: Clarendon Press.

Sharpe, L.J. 1973. "British and American Conceptions of Democracy." *British Journal of Political Science* 3: 1–28; 129–68.

Skocpol, Theda. 1992. *Protecting Mothers and Soldiers.* Cambridge, Mass.: Harvard University Press.

Skrentny, John David. 1996. *The Ironies of Affirmative Action: Politics, Culture and Justice in America.* Chicago: University of Chicago Press.

Smith, Rogers. 1993. "Beyond Tocqueville, Myrdal, and Hartz." *American Political Science Review* 87, no. 3:549–66.

Sniderman, Paul M., and Thomas Piazza. 1993. *The Scar of Race.* Cambridge, Mass.: Belknap Press.

Sombart, Werner. 1976. *Why Is There No Socialism in the United States?* Trans. Patricia M. Hocking and C.T. Husbands. London: Macmillan. First published in 1905.

Steinmo, Sven. 1995. "Why Is Government So Small in America?" *Governance* 8:303–34.

Stigler, George. 1986. *Regularities of Regulation.* London: David Hume Institute.

———. 1971. "The Theory of Economic Regulation." *Bell Journal of Economic and Management Science* 2:3–21.

Stouffer, Samuel. 1955. *Communism, Conformity and Civil Liberties.* New York: Doubleday.

Sullivan, John L., J.E. Pierson, and Gregory E. Marcus. 1982. *Political Tolerance and American Democracy.* Chicago: University of Chicago Press.

Thatcher, Margaret. 1993. *Downing Street Years.* New York: HarperCollins.

Thurber, James A., and Roger H. Davidson, eds. 1995. *Remaking Congress:*

Change and Stability in the 1990s. Washington, D.C.: CQ Press.

Tocqueville, Alexis de. 1948. *Democracy in America,* vols. I and II. New York: Knopf.

Tufte, Edward. 1978. *Political Control of the Economy*. Princeton: Princeton University Press.

Verba, Sidney, and Gary Orren. 1985. *Equality in America: The View from the Top*. Cambridge, Mass.: Harvard University Press.

Vogel, David. 1989. *Fluctuating Fortunes: The Political Power of Business in America*. New York: Basic Books.

Weaver, R. Kent, and Bert A. Rockman, eds. 1993. *Do Institutions Matter? Government Capabilities in the United States and Abroad*. Washington, D.C.: Brookings Institution.

Weidenbaum, Murray. 1983. *Regulatory Reform: A Report Card for the Reagan Administration*. St. Louis: Center for the Study of American Business.

———. 1979. "The Trend of Government Regulation of Business," paper prepared for the Hoover Institution Conference on Regulation, Stanford University, July.

Weidenbaum, Murray, and Robert DeFina. 1978. *The Costs of Federal Regulation of Economic Activity*. Washington, D.C.: American Enterprise Institute.

Wiebe, Robert. 1995. *Self Rule: A Cultural History of American Democracy*. Chicago: University of Chicago Press.

Wildavsky, Aaron, and Hugh Heclo. 1970. *The Private Government of Public Money*. London: Macmillan.

Wilensky, Harold. 1975. *The Welfare State and Equality: Structural and Ideological Roots of Public Expenditure*. Berkeley: University of California Press.

Wilson, Graham K. 1985. *The Politics of Safety and Health: Occupational Safety and Health in the United States and Britain*. Oxford: Clarendon Press.

Wilson, James Q. 1989. *Bureaucracy: What Government Agencies Do and Why They Do It*. New York: Basic Books.

———, ed. 1980. *The Politics of Regulation*. New York: Basic Books.

Witte, John F. 1985. *The Politics and Development of the Federal Income Tax*. Madison: University of Wisconsin Press.

Wolff, Edward N. 1996. "How the Pie Is Sliced: America's Growing Concentration of Wealth." In *Ticking Time Bombs: The New Conservative Assault on Democracy,* ed. Robert L. Kuttner. New York: New Press.

Young, M. Crawford, ed. 1993. *The Rising Tide of Cultural Pluralism: The Nation State at Bay?* Madison: University of Wisconsin Press.

Index

Index